THE ROYAL HORTICULTURAL SOCIETY
PRACTICAL GUIDES

CLIMBING PLANTS

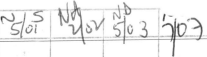

THE ROYAL HORTICULTURAL SOCIETY
PRACTICAL GUIDES

CLIMBING PLANTS

CHARLES CHESSHIRE

A Dorling Kindersley Book

Dorling [DK] Kindersley

LONDON, NEW YORK, SYDNEY, DELHI, PARIS, MUNICH AND JOHANNESBURG

SERIES EDITOR Annelise Evans
SERIES ART EDITOR Ursula Dawson
DTP DESIGNERS Louise Paddick, Louise Waller
PRODUCTION MANAGER Sarah Coltman

MANAGING EDITOR Anna Kruger
MANAGING ART EDITOR Lee Griffiths

Produced for Dorling Kindersley by

studio cactus ©

13 SOUTHGATE STREET WINCHESTER HAMPSHIRE SO23 9DZ

SENIOR EDITOR Jane Baldock
SENIOR DESIGNER Sharon Moore

First published in Great Britain in 2001 by
Dorling Kindersley Limited,
9 Henrietta Street,
Covent Garden, London WC2E 8PS

2 4 6 8 10 9 7 5 3

A CIP catalogue record for this book is available from the British Library

ISBN 0 7513 1293 2

Reproduced by Colourscan, Singapore
Printed and bound by Star Standard Industries PTE Ltd, Singapore

See our complete catalogue at

www.dk.com

CONTENTS

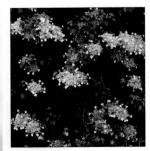

CLIMBING PLANTS IN THE GARDEN

WHAT IS A CLIMBER?

CLIMBING PLANTS DO NOT FORM a firm stem or trunk to support themselves. Instead, they scramble along the ground, often rooting themselves on the way, until they find a suitable object to climb, such as a wall or another plant. By climbing, the plant can reach more light and keep out of the reach of predators. Different climbers have evolved certain methods for attaching themselves to various surfaces, for example, ivy uses clinging stem roots, and clematis has twining stems.

USING CLIMBERS

Climbers are adventurous and opportunistic plants. Some are annuals, living for only one growing season, while others can make a permanent presence in the garden. The most common use of climbing plants is to cover walls and fences, but they can also be grown up and through other plants to make many interesting combinations. They can be grown in open soil or pots, on frameworks (such as arbours and arched tunnels), on obelisks, against trellis, or simply on a fence. Planting climbers against a building can enhance the beauty of a house or hide an unattractive aspect.

Even the very smallest of gardens can accommodate a climbing plant somewhere, for example, they can be used effectively in a container by a basement staircase or on a balcony or rooftop trailing along the railings.

◀ CONTAINER CLIMBER
Plumbago auriculata *grows in a copper tub against a wall where it can trail over the edge of the tub and be trained up against the wall.*

WHY CHOOSE CLIMBERS?

- In a small garden, climbers can clothe walls without taking up too much space.
- They can be grown over buildings and other structures to provide a screen, or over old and dead trees for a sculptural effect.
- Climbers can be grown over attractive frames, such as arches, pergolas, arbours, tunnels, obelisks, and simple canes.
- They can be grown over other plants to flower at a different time, extending the period of interest or creating unusual effects.

◀ A TUNNEL OF ROSES *This is a perfect way to capture the scent of roses on a garden walk.*

NATURAL HABIT

Climbing plants use different methods of attaching or entangling themselves with their hosts. The majority have twisting or twining growth that curls around a support like a snake wrapped around a branch. Others have specialized tendrils, such as the modified leaves of sweet peas (*Lathyrus*), which reach out to the nearest surface, such as a wire or a twig, and twist themselves around it to ensure good support.

In the case of clematis, the leaf itself can twist. Other plants, such as ivy and climbing hydrangea, use modified stem or aerial roots. These attach themselves to walls, rock-faces, or tree bark. Virginia creeper has adhesive pads at the ends of tendril-like growths that grip any surface.

> In nature, climbers rely on host plants for support

In this book we also refer to plants that are scandent. These are often borderline climbers because they are, in essence, shrubs that are very lax in growth, either forming a tangled mound when isolated or using the sturdy woody structure of a shrub or tree as support. By these means they attain the heights that other climbers may reach.

CLIMBERS WITH OTHER PLANTS

The majority of climbers in nature use other plants as support; some, like honeysuckles and bittersweet, can even strangle and kill their host plants in their endeavour to climb. Nevertheless, by carefully matching the vigour and climbing method of your climber to the vigour and habit of the host plant, you can create some of the finest garden sights with this managed "drapery".

In big gardens, a rampant rambling rose or *Clematis montana* will grow to over 10m (30ft), often tumbling and cascading their growth out of a tall tree. *Vitis coignetiae*, hops, wisteria, and Russian vine may also be grown through large, strong-growing trees, while ivies often climb naturally up trees. There is much debate regarding whether ivies should be discouraged from doing so, since they can damage their host, but an ivy-clad tree can be a wonderful sight in winter and provides nectar for bees in late autumn and a winter roosting place for birds. The size and strength of the host tree will also need to be taken into consideration; a vigorous climber may overwhelm a young or unhealthy tree.

On a lower level, less vigorous climbers can be trained over shrubs and through herbaceous borders. Large-flowered clematis and some honeysuckles can grace a large and vigorous shrub, such as lilac, philadelphus, cotinus, and evergreens, such as holly and a mature laurel. Plan combinations carefully to give colour after a shrub has finished flowering, or to have both climber and shrub flowering at the

MIXED PLANTING
The leaves of Vitis vinifera *'Purpurea' are perfect foils to the reddish-purple flowers of* Clematis viticella, *scrambling over an old tree stump.*

◀ CLIMBING HOP
The golden-leaved hop, Humulus lupulus 'Aureus', *is a vigorous climber that dies down each year and has attractive yellowish-green leaves in spring. Care must be taken that climbers do not damage buildings; in this situation, roof tiles may be lifted and guttering blocked or damaged.*

▼ CAMOUFLAGE
Wooden posts around a rubbish bin form a screening frame for climbers such as clematis.

same time. Annual climbers, such as nasturtiums and black-eyed Susans, can scramble through mixed borders of herbaceous plants and shrubs.

CLIMBERS FOR SCREENING

Climbing plants are often used with stunning results as screens or boundaries, providing privacy and focal points in the garden. Grown over trellises or wires attached to posts, climbers can be trained to cover most structures to soften the visual impact of a building or to screen unattractive objects such as rubbish bins. Evergreens are particularly effective in this role, providing year-round cover. Choose a climber to suit the form of the structure. If a climber is vigorous and grows to a height taller than the support, growth can fall back to the ground and become difficult to manage, or the plant may only flower at the top.

YEAR-ROUND INTEREST

To CREATE A WELL-PLANNED GARDEN with a wide variety of plants, careful consideration should be given to choosing a selection of plants that provide interest for most of the year. It may not be possible to have plants in flower all year round, but many climbers with evergreen leaves or decorative seedheads will be interesting over winter. In a small garden, where there is room for only one or two climbers, this choice is more critical.

EARLY INTEREST

In winter, although there are a few climbers that flower, the emphasis is on choosing an attractive evergreen. For cold areas, one reasonably hardy winter-flowering climber is *Clematis cirrhosa* and its varieties. Hardy down to −14°C (7°F), this evergreen carries creamy coloured bells; in 'Freckles', these are creamy-pink and heavily speckled with red inside. The flowers can tolerate a few degrees of frost and can be carried from late autumn until late winter. Bittersweet bears golden-yellow capsules on leafless branches into midwinter, and the seedheads of *Clematis tangutica* remain almost all winter long. *Jasminum polyanthum*, and some climbers usually grown as annuals, such as black-eyed Susan and cup and saucer plant, will flower through the winter in colder climates if they are grown in containers outside in summer, and overwintered in a conservatory with good light.

▲ FRAGRANT ELEGANCE
This wisteria hangs down from a balcony. Strategic planting allows the wisteria flowers to trail freely so that their fragrance can permeate a social space.

◄ SUBTLE SCENTS
Although extremely vigorous, with careful pruning Clematis montana *can be trained over an arch, where its sweet almond scent can be appreciated as you pass underneath.*

◄ A SHADY BENCH
In summer, this vine, Vitis coignetiae, *with its huge leaves will provide welcome shade and a cool spot in which to sit.*

▼ AFTERNOON SIESTA
Morning glory flowers open in the morning and close by midday, especially in hot sun. A rapid-growing annual, morning glory's twining growth will climb up walls on wire supports or over shrubs and small trees, but this climber can be very invasive in warmer climates.

For spring interest, *Clematis alpina* and *C. macropetala* have pendulous flowers in a range of colours from white to pink, purple, and blue, followed by *C. montana,* which flowers into early summer. By far the most impressive spring climber, however, is wisteria, whose buds fatten to the point just before opening when they are prone to frost damage. Some wisterias have the advantage of flowering again later in summer, especially the *W. sinensis* varieties.

LATER BLOOMS

Summer is the main season for climbers, when jasmine, honeysuckle, and roses are in flower. Most rambler roses bloom for only three or four weeks, but a number of modern climbers repeat-flower throughout the summer. As the first roses fade, many late-flowering clematis begin, such as *C. viticella* (purples, pinks, and whites) and *C. tangutica* (yellow). Cape leadwort flowers throughout the summer into autumn, while the solanums, relatives of the potato, flower from early summer in both white and blue-purple.

SUMMER COLOUR

Summer is the time when most of the annual climbers come into full flower. Nasturtiums tumble in a trail of oranges, reds, and yellows; black-eyed Susans have yellow flowers with black centres; morning glories are covered with blue trumpets; and sweet peas are ready for picking. The curious pendulous red flowers of rhodochitons will continue right into autumn.

In late summer, the climbing hydrangea carries its flattened heads of creamy-white flowers, as do schizophragmas and pileostegias. Russian vine, or mile-a-minute, is covered in a spectacular cloud of small white flowers at this time.

In autumn, many climbers develop vivid red and burgundy foliage, such as Virginia creeper and Boston ivy, and the vines *Vitis coignetiae* and *V. vinifera* 'Purpurea'. *Ampelopsis glandulosa* var. *brevipedunculata* bears small bunches of blue berries.

EVERGREEN FAVOURITES

The finest of the evergreen flowering climbers tend to be less than fully hardy. The best site for most of these is either on a sunny wall in a sheltered garden or, in colder climates, in a conservatory, where the foliage is protected from the ravages of winter. A good example is holboellias, with their lush foliage, and fragrant flowers that appear in early spring.

For a cool site in a sheltered garden with acid soil, *Berberidopsis corallina* has bold, dark green foliage and red berry-like

> Autumn is the season for fruits, such as grapes, gourds, and rosehips

flowers in summer. *Trachelospermum jasminoides* has tidy evergreen foliage and small, white, scented flowers in summer.

Of the more hardy evergreens, *Lonicera japonica* is a good all-rounder, with small, cream-coloured, fragrant flowers. It blooms in full sun or partial shade, but it can be invasive in warmer areas. For cold regions, the ivies and euonymus provide background foliage. Many clematis will grow through these evergreens to give the impression that they are flowering. *Clematis viticella* is one of the best because, being hard pruned in winter, its bare, woody growth will not encumber the evergreens.

FOLIAGE PLANTS

The golden hop, *Humulus lupulus* 'Aureus', is grown solely for its bold, golden lime-green foliage in early summer. Ivy, *Euonymus fortunei*, *Ficus pumila*, and *Cissus striata*

IVY GATEWAY
Large-leaved forms of the ivy Hedera colchica *enjoy shady positions that can be quite dry. The leaves are evergreen and offer a welcome cheer in winter, especially this cream-edged variegated form.*

▲ FLUFFY SEEDHEADS
*Some clematis have fluffy
seedheads that last until winter.
Clematis tangutica has yellow
bells in summer, often at the
same time as the seedheads.*

◀ CHANGING COLOUR
*A number of vines change
to fabulous hues in autumn.
Here* Vitis coignetiae *can cover
an old tree or building to
bring it alive for a few weeks.*

are all evergreens with insignificant flowers, but whose leaves offer the winter garden some colour. The vibrant leaves of *Actinidia kolomikta* look as if they have been splashed with pink and white paint. Virginia creeper and Boston ivy – both deciduous – are also grown for their attractive foliage, especially for their blazing autumn colours.

SEASONAL HIGHLIGHTS

Some plants have more than one main visual quality. *Vitis vinifera* and its varieties 'Purpurea' and 'Incana' have white felt covering the leaves in spring; in summer, this felt turns purple on the former and grey-green on the latter. Both then turn a wonderful claret-purple in the autumn, and often bear bunches of tart but edible grapes. The flowering of *Clematis macropetala* is followed by silvery, fluffy seedheads, and in late summer, C. 'Bill Mackenzie' carries both flowers and seedheads at the same time. The seedheads continue to provide attractive visual interest in midwinter.

Some rambling roses, such as 'The Garland', have bunches of orange-red hips in autumn, which remain well into winter until the birds eat them. 'New Dawn' is one of the best all-round climbing roses, with its shell-pink flowers carried over much of the summer, some hips, and its good glossy foliage.

Wisteria, although deciduous, has wonderful evocatively twisting trunks and masses of beautiful scented flowers, while the leaves in some forms turn a lovely butter-yellow in autumn.

Climbers that die down each winter include herbaceous perennials such as hops, sweet peas, some clematis, dicentras, Dutchman's pipe, bomareas, Chilean glory flower, and nasturtium. For this reason, they are not so suitable for screening, but their reappearance every spring does add an element of surprise to any garden scheme. Mostly late flowering, they can be encouraged to grow through spring flowering shrubs to prolong their interest.

Suiting the Garden Conditions

ALTHOUGH MANY CLIMBERS are easy to grow under a range of conditions, it is important to try to match their needs as closely as possible to achieve the best results. In some cases, if these needs are ignored, the plants will grow poorly, or even die. The main points to consider are a plant's hardiness (dealt with in the directory, *see pp.57–77*), its preferred soil type, the degree of moisture and light it requires, and the amount of exposure to winds that it can tolerate.

Soil Types

There are many types of soil, ranging between the two extremes of heavy clay, which is generally alkaline, and light sand, which is usually acid. Sandy soils tend to be very free-draining and infertile, so for plants requiring moisture and high fertility, add plenty of organic matter in the form of rotted manure. Mulching with bark, rotted manure, or gravel will help to conserve moisture, reflect heat away from the root system, and deter weeds that could otherwise compete for valuable moisture.

Honeysuckles are an example of how varied the requirements of closely related plants can be. All honeysuckles are happy in a good loamy soil, rich in organic matter with plenty of moisture available during the

CLIMBING HYDRANGEA
Ideally suited to a shady wall in almost any kind of reasonable soil, this self-clinging hydrangea produces its flattened white flowerheads in summer.

> The ideal soil type
> for most garden plants
> is a good loam

growing season, but while *Lonicera periclymenum* is happiest on clay, *L. etrusca* prefers drier and hotter conditions and *L. japonica* enjoys light, sandy soil. All honeysuckles are fairly shallow rooted and prefer their roots to be kept cool.

Few climbers tolerate very wet growing conditions, but roses, honeysuckles, and climbing hydrangea all enjoy heavy clay soils once they have become well established. Delicate evergreens suffer in heavy clay soils that do not drain freely in winter. Waterlogging prevents leaves from functioning properly, especially if the ground is cold or frozen, with the result that plants wilt and rot at the roots.

Climbers that tolerate a light, sandy soil include campsis, solanums, and lobster claws. Bignonias, Virginia creeper, holboellias, and Boston ivy all grow well in most soil types, but thrive in these

▲ FERTILE SOILS
Once established, honeysuckle, roses, and clematis thrive on heavy clay, which is more moisture-retentive and fertile than sandy soil.

▶ A CLIMBER FOR SANDY SOILS
A superb, vigorous, self-clinging climber, Campsis grandiflora is happy in sandy soils, even quite close to the sea.

conditions. Some plants grow best in moisture retentive, acidic soils, including *Akebia quinata*, pileostegias, *Tropaeolum speciosum*, *Berberidopsis corallina*, and lapagerias. In alkaline conditions, the latter two plants grow weakly, with yellow leaves. Plants that prefer alkaline soils may tolerate slightly acid ones, but, if not, it is easier to add lime to neutralize the soil than to make a soil acidic. Clematis thrives in nature on chalky, alkaline soils, and in a garden situation will grow in all but the most acid soils. On the whole, these climbers prefer moisture retentive soils.

A few climbers can withstand exposure to cold and winds, for example, *Clematis alpina*, ivy, climbing hydrangea, and most of the rambler roses.

Seaside gardens have a milder climate than inland areas, but exposure to salt-laden winds can damage plants. After a gale or storm, washing down the plants with fresh water will minimize the scorching effect. Ivy, berberidopsis, some clematis species, lobster claw, Chilean glory flower, euonymus, Russian vine (*Fallopia*), climbing hydrangea, muehlenbeckias, solanums, and many honeysuckles will tolerate seaside exposure to some degree.

GOOD ALL-ROUNDERS

These good all-rounders tolerate a wide range of soil types and garden conditions.
Actinidia kolomikta
Ampelopsis glandulosa var. *brevipedunculata*
Clematis alpina (large-flowered hybrids)
Euonymus fortunei var. *radicans*
Hedera
Humulus lupulus
Jasminum officinale and *J. polyanthum*
Lonicera (most)
Muehlenbeckia
Parthenocissus quinquefolia
Vitis (most)

FULL SUN AND PARTIAL SHADE

Plants vary considerably in their light requirements. Some will scorch when exposed to full sun, particularly at midday, while others need plenty of sun to promote flowering, to ripen their fruit, and to develop their growth so as to be hardy enough for the winter. In different parts of the world, the intensity of the sun varies in summer and winter. A plant that prefers dappled shade where the sun is strong may be happy in full sun in cooler climates, where the sun is less intense.

Climbers are often planted against walls, where the warmth of the sun is intensified. White walls reflect more light, which may be too much for some plants. Others, such as bougainvilleas, enjoy as much sun as they can get. In winter, walls retain heat during the day and release a small amount at night, protecting plants from frosts. Careful thought must be given to moisture levels however, since the base of walls can be dry.

Consideration must be given to the degree of shade. The shade on the wall of a house that faces away from the sun may not be as dense as that under a tree, and trees vary considerably as to the amount of shade they cast. Sycamore and beech, for instance, often create shade too deep for most plants, while their roots make conditions too dry. Ivy and *Euonymus fortunei*, however, are good plants for deep shade, and, once established, will also tolerate dry conditions.

The shade of trees like common oak, sweet chestnut, and birch is lighter and the roots of the trees much deeper. These trees provide excellent shade for climbers such as honeysuckle, schizophragmas, and

◄ SHADY SPACES
A gold-splashed Hedera helix *'Goldheart' and a climbing hydrangea are good choices for a shady wall.*

▼ SUN-LOVING SWEET PEA
Plenty of sunshine, a good moist root run, and frequent cutting will keep fragrant sweet peas flowering throughout most of summer.

LIGHT REQUIREMENTS OF PLANTS

FOR FULL SUN
Actinidia
Akebia
Ampelopsis
Aristolochia
*Bignonia**
*Billardiera**
Bomarea
*Bougainvillea**
Campsis
Clematis armandii
Clematis cirrhosa
*Clematis
  rehderiana*
*Clianthus**
*Cobaea**
Cucurbita
Dicentra
*Dregea**
Eccremocarpus
Fallopia
Gelsemium
*Ipomoea**
Jasminum

Lathyrus
Lonicera especially
Lonicera etrusca
Lonicera ×
  tellmanniana
*Lonicera
  tragophylla*
Muehlenbeckia
Parthenocissus
*Passiflora**
Pileostegia
*Plumbago**
Rhodochiton
Rosa
Rubus
Schizophragma
Solanum
*Sollya**
*Thunbergia**
Trachelospermum
Tweedia
Vitis
Wisteria

**FOR PARTIAL
SHADE**
Aristolochia
*Berberidopsis**
Celastrus
Clematis viticella
*Cobaea**
Eccremocarpus
Euonymus
Fallopia
Ficus pumila
Hedera
*Holboellia**
Humulus lupulus
  'Aureus'
*Lapageria**
Lonicera
Muehlenbeckia
Parthenocissus
Rubus
Schisandra
Schizophragma
Tropaeolum

**FOR SHADE AND
SUNLESS WALLS**
*Cissus striata**
Clematis alpina,
*Clematis
  macropetala*
Euonymus fortunei
Hedera
Holboellia
*Hydrangea
  anomola* subsp.
  petiolaris
Parthenocissus
Rosa 'Madame
  Alfred Carrière',
  'Mermaid', 'New
  Dawn', 'Noisette
  Carnée'

*Denotes not
reliably hardy

bittersweet. It is important to remember, however, that it may not be possible to see a climber's flowers until it has reached a good height. Many climbers may start off life in the deep shade of a tree but, as they climb up their host, they find more and more light in the open canopy of the tree. Meanwhile, some climbers deliberately planted on the shady side of a tree may well find their way to the sunny side, where the flowers may be hidden from view.

Although most prefer full sun, some climbing and rambling roses are suitable for growing on a north wall, as are some of the paler, large-flowered clematis, whose colours fade in bright sunlight.

DEGREES OF SHADE
Schizophragma integrifolium *will grow well in shade, but too much shade will stop it from flowering. Shade intensity will vary depending on the strength of the sun and the climate of your region.*

FRAGRANT CLIMBERS

CLIMBING PLANTS THAT HAVE SCENTED FLOWERS are ideal for planting around doorways or arches and for hanging strategically over benches, where their impact can be so readily and happily enjoyed. Fortunately, there are many fragrant climbing plants from which to choose. Scent in plants transcends colour and form: relatively insignificant blooms can exude a sweet smell that fills the air all around and can even perfume the house through open windows.

FRAGRANT FAVOURITES

Some of the best-loved plants are fragrant climbers such as roses, jasmine, and honeysuckle, but there are others, such as wisteria and clematis, and the delicately scented sweet pea, that add much to a garden if placed where their scent can carry.

Many rambler roses are also fragrant. 'Francis E. Lester' has been used in the hybridizing of many ramblers, and is a useful rambler for colonizing a wild garden. The fragrance of a rambler in flower can carry over distances of up to 50m (160ft).

SCENTS FOR THE GARDEN

Trachelospermums are evergreen climbers with masses of periwinkle-like flowers in summer, accompanied by a wonderful scent. *T. jasminoides* and *T. asiaticum* are very similar in character, but the latter has smaller leaves and is marginally hardier. Their tidy growth makes them ideal for planting near doorways. *Holboellia coriacea* is also evergreen, with small, greenish-white flowers. Intensely fragrant, their strong scent can carry across a garden and through windows into the house.

HONEYSUCKLE POST
A honeysuckle can be twined around a stone post but will need loops of wire to hold it in place. Plant more than one variety to extend the flowering season and to add different colour tones to the feature, but note that some honeysuckles are not fragrant.

▲ FRAGRANT BLOOMS
If well placed, the heady scent of wisteria can carry quite long distances. With careful pruning, wisteria will produce a larger quantity of flowers.

◀ GARDEN HAVEN
A scented bench is an enticing garden feature. Be careful to prune roses to avoid them snagging sitters with their thorns. Other fragrant plants can be planted on the ground around the bench so that their perfume may be released by people approaching.

Not all honeysuckles are fragrant. Those derived from *Lonicera periclymenum* and *L. japonica* are scented and are at their strongest in the evening. *Jasminum officinale* and *J. polyanthum* are both relatively hardy and carry a sweet perfume. Meanwhile, *Dregea sinensis* has a delicate scent, but should be positioned carefully to ensure it is not overwhelmed with more potent fragrances. Wisteria, especially *W. sinensis*, has a heady perfume. When it is trained on a house wall, where pruning (*see pp.42–44*) has encouraged it to flower more densely, the scent may waft back into the house through open doors and windows.

Clematis

These popular climbers can offer a garden some wonderful scents. *Clematis montana* has a fragrance of almonds but the cultivars vary in their intensity. 'Odorata' and 'Fragrant Spring' are particularly well-scented. In summer, *C. flammula* and its

hybrid *C.* × *triternata* 'Rubromarginata' are both covered in clouds of starry white and purple flowers, and their fragrance permeates a garden. In late summer, *C. rehderiana* has creamy-coloured, cowslip-scented flowers.

FRAGRANT ROSES

CLIMBING ROSES	RAMBLING ROSES
'Alister Stella Gray'	'Albéric Barbier'
'Climbing Etoile de Hollande'	'Albertine'
'Climbing Lady Hillingdon'	'Bobbie James'
'Gloire de Dijon'	'Francis E. Lester'
'Guinée'	'Kew Rambler'
'Lawrence Johnston'	'La Mortola'
'Madame Alfred Carrière'	'Noisette Carnée'
'Madame Grégoire Staechelin'	'Paul's Himalayan Musk'
'Maigold'	'Phyllis Bide'
'New Dawn'	'Rambling Rector'
	'Seagull'
	'The Garland'
	'Veilchenblau'

CLIMBERS FOR CONTAINERS

Planting climbers in pots can be very effective, particularly on patios and balustrades, where annual and perennial climbers can climb canes or specially designed frames. Containers have the advantage of allowing you to grow plants with specific requirements in areas where they will not grow in the ground; the acid-loving Chilean bellflower, for example, can be potted in an alkaline garden. In cold areas, tender container plants can be moved into greenhouses or conservatories before the frosts, then placed outside in summer.

ANNUALS IN POTS

All the annual climbers mentioned in this book are suitable for growing in containers, as long as the container is large enough to accommodate them for the whole growing season. Cup and saucer plants have considerable vigour and can be trained to grow over a fence or up the side of a house. Black-eyed susan, rhodochitons, and sweet peas would all be ideal for training over tripods and obelisks sunk into the container. Alternatively, nasturtiums and gourds can be planted in large tubs and allowed to trail, but they may spread up to 3m (10ft) over the ground (*see* Climbers for ground cover *p.25*). Both are heavy feeders, which means that they should be fertilized regularly throughout the season and watered frequently.

MOBILE DISPLAYS
Thunbergia alata *is a brightly coloured climber that is an annual in cold climates. It can be brought indoors before frosts to flower in winter.*

RECOMMENDED

Bougainvillea
Clematis alpina and
Clematis macropetala types
Clematis large-flowered and
  compact forms
Clematis viticella will need
  to have growth spiralled
Jasminium
Passiflora can be grown in
  containers over frames
Plumbago, grown for its
  succession of blue flowers
Rhodochiton
Trachelospermum

▲ CONTAINERS FOR BALCONIES
Evergreen and elegant in its trailing habit, this variegated ivy softens the severity of the railings and can be left over winter after the annual flowers have been removed.

◄ POTTED SCENTS
Easily grown in a pot, Jasminum officinale *can be moved to a prominent position when in flower where its fragrance can be enjoyed.*

PERENNIALS IN POTS

As perennial climbers may be inhabiting the same pot for extended periods, the choice of soil for the container is important. In general, use a compost that is not too light or heavy, but retains moisture well – containers tend to dry out quickly. Check the individual requirements of the plant, such as whether it prefers an acid soil or not.

A good choice for containers is clematis and there are many suitable kinds to choose between. For spring flowers try a *Clematis alpina* or *C. macropetala*. These need large pots and frequent feeding, but may be placed in a shady position, where they will need less watering. Large-flowered varieties for both early and late summer flowering need to be chosen carefully, both for their length of flowering and for the style of their growth.

Many clematis have very lanky growth, with the flowers borne near the top of the plant. If the growth is spiralled around a tripod in the winter, the flowers will be carried more evenly over the plant, but there are some such as 'Niobe' (red) and 'The Bride' (creamy-white) that have naturally compact growth and a long flowering season. 'Prince Charles' (blue) is tall growing but also has a long season. Herbaceous clematis, such as 'Arabella', with small, blue, star-shaped flowers carried over the whole summer, make excellent pot plants but need tying because they do not have tendrils to grasp supports.

Maintain a colourful display with frequent feeding and watering

Trachelospermums carry white, fragrant, periwinkle-like flowers in early summer, while jasmine makes an excellent pot plant – both *Jasminum polyanthum* and *J. officinale* are suitable. Passion flower grows well in containers but *Passiflora caerulea* is vigorous and may outgrow even a large pot within a few years. Honeysuckle and wisteria can be grown in large pots but may need to be planted out after a few years.

CLIMBERS AS FEATURES

APART FROM GROWING CLIMBERS through other plants, another popular way of training climbing plants is over structures designed to accommodate them. On some, such as arbours and pergolas, the plants are used to offer shade during the summer months. Other supports, such as obelisks, can be used in a garden to provide a vertical accent in a border. Even if they are bare during the winter months, many structures can be very attractive in their own right.

ARBOURS AND PERGOLAS

Arbours and pergolas are fairly similar and can both be used to create stunning displays of colourful, fragrant climbers. An arbour is a shady retreat, sometimes made of living trees but more often made of wood or wrought iron. It can be a particularly attractive feature when

> Arches over pathways should be wide enough to allow for growth

covered with a rambling rose or *Clematis montana*, while the plants also serve to provide shade. A pergola more often describes a structure that is attached to the house to provide shade in summer. This is the perfect support for a grape vine, whose fruits will hang down, or a

wisteria, whose long flower-chains can drape between the cross beams. A pergola can also be a walkway of posts with wires strung between them, and offers a chance to plant plenty of fragrant climbers such as roses, honeysuckles, clematis, and sweet peas. Walkways are often accompanied by narrow borders on either side, where underplantings of herbaceous plants and annuals can complete a wonderful, colourful garden scene.

ARCHES

For displaying climbing plants, arches are similar to both arbours and pergolas, but are especially effective when placed over gateways where they can be festooned with fragrant climbers. Roses, clematis, and honeysuckle are all ideal for training over arches. Annual climbers such as sweet peas, in complementary colours, can be grown up the lower bare stems of roses on an arch.

DECORATIVE BEANS
Runner beans have attractive red and white flowers and can be grown in the flower garden and underplanted with perennials and annuals. Grow them up a trellis, rope net, arch, or the traditional tripod of canes.

◀ CREATING SHADE
*Pergolas are useful
for providing shade
over terraces or
patios in summer.
You will need to
control the ivy's
growth in order to
prevent it blocking
gutters and
encroaching on
adjoining buildings.*

▼ SCENTED ARCH
*Fragrant climbers
such as honeysuckle
are especially suitable
for growing over
arches. Planting
different varieties on
each side of the arch
will extend the
flowering season.*

OBELISKS AND PYRAMIDS

These are usually four-sided, tapering
pillars, usually made of wood or wrought
iron. All kinds of climbers can be grown
over these, but care must be taken to match
the height of the climber to the structure. If
the structure is too short, for example, a
vigorous plant can become difficult to
train. When plants are getting too tall, you
can make them "fit" by spiralling new,
flexible growth around the support. Large-
flowered clematis, honeysuckles and
rambling roses can all be tied in like this.

Simple imitations can be made by tying
together a "wigwam" of canes, poles, or
twigs. These can be taken down during the
winter months if they are used for annual
climbers or hard-pruned ones. It is also
possible to buy more intricate versions
made of willow and bamboo.

CLIMBERS TRAINED AS TOPIARY

It can take years to establish a clipped topiary to the shape you want, but by using a wire cage it is possible to train climbing plants, especially evergreens, to achieve a topiary effect in a much shorter time. There are many wire frames available to buy, from simple globes to intricate animal shapes.

Some frameworks are large enough to be stuffed with soil that is held in place using netting, plastic, and moss. Small climbers can then be planted into the topiary frame, although a system must be devised to ensure that the plants are successfully watered. Wire stakes can also be plunged into pots or flower beds to form a frame for topiary.

Ivy is the most common plant used for topiary. The small-leaved varieties are the best for small designs, while a larger-leaved and more vigorous ones could be used to create topiary as tall as 5m (15ft). Other plants suitable for topiary include jasmine, *Euonymus fortunei*, muehlenbeckias, trachelospermums, and *Cissus striata*.

▲ BOSTON IVY BASKETS
Parthenocissus tricuspidata *in a hanging basket is best grown in partial shade where it will not dry out too much. Feed well and it may last in a basket for a few years.*

◀ IVY TOPIARY
A spiral, a two-ball, and a pyramid show the versatility of ivy as a plant that can be trained easily into many shapes. Evergreen and often variegated, shaped ivy in pots can be placed for year-round interest.

GROUND COVER

The most effective climbing plants for complete ground cover are ivy and *Euonymus fortunei*, since they also root wherever the stems touch the ground. Plants like ivy, however, do tend to climb up any other plant or surface that they encounter, although Irish ivy usually stays on the level.

Clematis, nasturtiums, rambling roses, and climbing hydrangea can look very effective growing over the ground alone or among other plants. Pileostegias and

---

> ## Trailing plants with decorative fruits provide stunning effects

---

schizophragmas also provide good ground cover and the former particularly enjoys cool, shady positions.

Heavy gourds need to be grown on the level because no support could hold the fruit without either the fruit or the support breaking. Ornamental gourds can be allowed to trail attractively through the vegetable garden, often producing their fruit in amongst the other plants.

SOFTENING EDGES

Ivy is extremely good at disguising and softening the sides of steps, which can be visually stark or severe. It can be trained across the face of the riser and clipped regularly to control its growth.

TRAILING CLIMBERS

FOR WINDOWBOXES
Hedera helix and varieties
Some dwarf variegated ivies

FOR LARGE POTS
Tropaeolum

FOR TRAILING DOWN SLOPES OR HIGH WALLS
Akebia quinata
Clematis montana
Clematis alpina
Clematis viticella
Clematis texensis
Hedera helix (most)
Humulus lupulus 'Aureus'
Parthenocissus
Passiflora
Rosa rambling types
Trachelospermum
Vitis coignetiae
Vitis vinifera

CLIMBERS FOR BUILDINGS

THE MORE VIGOROUS CLIMBERS can be very helpful plants for covering unsightly buildings or simply enhancing plain architecture. They can be used to soften hard edges or merely to decorate a façade with beautiful flowers. Brick and stone buildings are more suited to being covered than more vulnerable timber ones, and some climbing plants can be a menace when planted inappropriately, so care must be taken when making a selection.

ENHANCING A BUILDING

Disguising ugly buildings can be done by planting climbers that do not need support, such as Virginia creeper or Boston ivy. This is important if the building is very tall or if attaching wires or trellis would be awkward. Other self-clinging vines, such as ivies and pileostegias, can all be considered, although the aerial roots of some ivies can break up soft plaster and loose mortar, allowing damp into the building. Roots can cling to the paintwork around windows and doors, so when the plant is removed, the paint comes away with it. Common ivy is a particular culprit and must be kept clear of gutters, roofs, windows, and doorways.

Russian vine, or mile-a-minute, is very popular for covering old sheds, often submerging them altogether, but this twining vine can block gutters and undermine tiles,

FRAGRANT FAÇADE
Many climbing roses have simple upright growth that makes them suitable for house walls, where the fragrant blooms can be enjoyed from open windows. Take full advantage of a warm sheltered wall to grow some of the more tender climbing Hybrid Teas. Feeding, good pruning, and deadheading will keep them healthy and flowering for a long time. Use a ladder or a long-handled pruner to reach inaccessible areas of the plant.

lifting them up as the stems expand. Wisteria can look wonderful with its pendulous flowers hanging down the side of a house and over doorways, but it has a strong twining action that can wrap itself around gutters and drainpipes and wrench them from their supports. *Clematis montana* and its varieties can also be both beautiful and a problem if left unchecked. With correct maintenance and pruning, however, these plants can all be used to great effect.

Climbing and rambling roses, jasmine, *Clematis armandii*, and honeysuckle can all be grown on house walls, where their fragrance can carry into the house itself, but supports strong enough to hold them must be put up at planting time.

SCREENING WITH CLIMBERS

Climbing plants can be used for screening by training them over fences and sturdy trellis. Suitable fast-growing species include Russian vine and *Clematis montana*. Some climbers, like Boston ivy and climbing hydrangea, although tall-growing, are quite slow in the first few years of growth.

▲ DECORATIVE DISGUISE
Although good at providing camouflage, wisteria can cause damage to drainpipes and roofs if not kept under control.

▼ CLIMBING STAIRS
An outdoor staircase provides a great opportunity for training climbers up an existing structure from which they can trail down.

CLIMBERS FOR CONSERVATORIES

THE PERFECT PLACE FOR GROWING tender climbers that would find it too cold outside is in a conservatory. Such a garden and living space is ideal for overwintering tender pot-grown climbing plants, which can then be placed outside during the summer to be enjoyed in the garden. Conservatories can also double as a greenhouse, and are useful for starting off seedlings of annual climbers, before they are planted out in late spring once the threat of frost has passed.

SHADING AND VENTILATION

Conservatories will vary in the environment they offer, according to which aspect they face and how much winter heating is available. If they are an extension of the living quarters of the house, they may have a very dry atmosphere, and if they face the sun they may stay pleasantly mild in winter but become exceedingly hot in summer. Care must be taken to provide conservatory plants with a reliable system of watering, and good ventilation or shading, or both.

Automatic ventilation systems that monitor and respond to the change in temperature are useful in preserving a constant environment, and some need no electricity to operate them. For a frost-free conservatory or greenhouse, you can install an electric heater with a frost-sensitive thermostat – this will gauge the temperature and automatically switch the heater on when it sinks to a few degrees above freezing.

In a greenhouse, you can train grape vines under the glazed roof, which will offer natural shade to both people and

> In a bright and sunny conservatory, climbers provide natural shade

plants. Alternatively, consider positioning a conservatory so that it receives only a minimum of sun, or install blinds that can be manually or automatically operated.

While *Jasminum polyanthum* will last much longer in flower if given some shade when the buds open, many conservatory plants, like bougainvilleas, will enjoy as much sun as you can offer, and particularly thrive in the heat of humid conservatories.

One climber that does not demand much heat is the grape vine. In a cold greenhouse it is possible to cultivate grape varieties that would not ripen successfully outside.

CONSERVATORY CLIMBER
Although tolerant of light frosts,
Lapageria rosea *var.* albiflora *is best grown in a greenhouse or conservatory. It should be given a moist position, with warm shade. In a greenhouse, plant it under a trained grape vine, where it will be shaded in summer.*

◄ GREENHOUSE GRAPES
In a cool climate, grape vines can be trained along wires under the roof of a greenhouse. They will need summer as well as winter pruning to allow light in and to give room for the fruits to develop. In a conservatory you may need to spray for pests and diseases.

TENDER CLIMBERS

Some conservatories and greenhouses have beds of soil in them that can be planted more or less permanently, especially if they are of the lean-to kind, which will often offer a whole house wall to adorn with climbers. Usually, however, plants for conservatories are all grown in pots. This has the advantage of allowing plants to be easily moved indoors or outdoors when required. Fragrant plants, such as *Holboellia coriacae*, for example, can be brought inside so that their perfume can be readily enjoyed in the close confines of the conservatory. Jasmine is perhaps the most popular conservatory plant, although hardy jasmines also grow well outdoors.

Within the somewhat closed atmosphere of a conservatory, however, the build up of pests and diseases can be a problem. If your conservatory is also a living area, this can be unpleasant, so it is important to plan before you plant. Whitefly, scale insects, woolly aphids, red spider mites, and

mildews can all ruin good plants. Plants in pots are easily dealt with because they can be taken outside and sprayed or cleaned off, except in freezing weather.

Treatment becomes a greater problem with more permanent plants such as grape vines, which are very prone to a wide variety of pests and diseases and have to be treated *in situ*.

CONSERVATORY CLIMBERS

Fast-growing plants for conservatories in colder climates, or for verandahs in more temperate regions

Actinidia deliciosa
Bignonia
Billardiera
Bomarea
Bougainvillea
Clematis
Clianthus
Dregea
Eccremocarpus
Holboellia
Jasminum polyanthum
Lapageria rosea
Plumbago auriculata
Rhodochiton
Sollya
Thunbergia
Trachelospermum
Tweedia caerulea
Vitis vinifera

LOOKING AFTER CLIMBING PLANTS

CHOOSING HEALTHY PLANTS

M OST PLANTS THESE DAYS are bought in containers, although some mail-order plants are sent bare-root. Bare-root plants should be checked for good healthy root systems and planted immediately, either into a container prior to planting out, directly into a nursery bed, or in their final position. If you are buying a plant in a container, always check it carefully first in order to assess whether or not it is in good health.

WHAT TO LOOK FOR

Before you buy, make sure the leaves are in good condition and that there are signs of new growth. For dormant or deciduous plants, check the previous season's growth. Ask the seller to remove the pot – roots that have only just reached the sides of the pot indicate the plant is ready for planting out. Pot-bound plants (those whose roots have grown around the inside of the container) should be rejected. A small healthy plant is a better buy than a larger pot-bound one.

BUYING TIPS
• Check foliage: yellowing leaves may mean a neglected plant or poor growing conditions.
• Choose a plant that is not yet in flower.
• Choose a bushy specimen with evenly spaced branches.
• If buying by mail order, find out how the plants are packed and delivered.
• Roots should be firm and well-developed, with some fibrous growth.

▶ HONEYSUCKLE IN POT
Large plants may not always be as satisfactory as smaller plants because they will take longer to adjust when first planted out.

COLOUR AND FRAGRANCE *Sweet pea, climbing rose, and clematis provide long-lasting flowers.*

GETTING THE MOST FROM CLIMBERS

MANY OF US ARE TEMPTED TO BUY PLANTS ON IMPULSE, or are given them by friends, without knowing where to plant them or what conditions they prefer. Impulse decisions should be avoided however. It is always advisable to establish where you need a climber first, and, having checked the aspect and soil of the area, to then find a plant that will thrive in such conditions. Some plants are much more adaptable than others.

CHOOSING A CLIMBER

Roses and honeysuckles are generally very adaptable to different conditions, while some climbers, like lime-hating berberidopsis, require specific soil types and plenty of moisture. If you are planting next to a wall, be aware that some plants have climbing habits that can cause damage to brickwork, for example, the clinging stem roots of ivy.

Strong, new growth

A GOOD EXAMPLE
This parthenocissus has strong stems and plenty of healthy foliage all the way up. The leaves are a dense green colour.

PLANT REQUIREMENTS
• Soil types: some plants like acid soils and others are happier in more alkaline soils.
• Sun/shade: in colder climates, full sun may be ideal for a particular plant, yet in hotter climes, full or partial shade may be more suitable.
• Water: some plants like almost dry soils while others need moisture at all times.
• Exposure: some plants will tolerate windy conditions while others wither in drying or cold winds. Salt-tolerance is vital by the sea.

Lush foliage is a good sign

The plant looks settled in its pot and the compost is free of algae and weeds.

PREPARING THE GROUND

Before planting, make sure that the ground is well prepared. If you have chosen a grassed area, remove any turf within a 50cm (20in) diameter of the intended position of the new plant, since grass will compete for valuable nutrients and water. There is also the danger that plants may be damaged by lawn cutting equipment like mowers and trimmers.

▶ DIGGING A PLANTING HOLE
The adjacent ground must be dug deeply with plenty of rotted organic matter like garden compost, rotted manure, or soil improver mixed in. Ensure that the drainage is good.

▲ MANURE
Any organic matter must be rotted down before you dig it in or use it as a mulch.

PLANTING CALENDAR

SPRING

- The ideal time for planting container-grown climbers into the ground.
- Early spring is fine for planting bare-root plants if they are well watered in.
- Ensure that new plants gradually get used to outdoor temperatures. Protect any soft growth that may be prone to late frosts by keeping plants in a green-house, or indoors overnight. Plant out in late spring.
- Hardy annuals, such as sweet peas and nasturtiums, can be planted out or direct sown in spring.
- Hard prune late summer-flowering climbers, removing any dead, diseased, or damaged wood.
- As plants begin to bud up, feed them with a top-dressing of rotted manure or a concentrated fertilizer. Liquid feed container plants.
- Sow half-hardy or tender annuals in a heated propagating frame or greenhouse (in warmer climates, place in a sheltered position). Prick out seedlings and pot into small pots.
- Mulch plants that enjoy moisture with a 5cm (2in) layer of bark or compost.
- Tie in young stems as they develop.
- Spray roses for diseases like black spot and rust.

SUMMER

- Plant out half-hardy and tender annual climbers in the garden after the frosts. If they have been in a heated greenhouse, harden off by introducing them slowly to the outdoor conditions.
- Water newly planted climbers every day if necessary, especially if pot grown and in full sun. Clematis particularly need plenty of water.
- Deadhead, removing faded flower shoots of climbing roses and early large-flowered clematis to encourage later flowers.
- Pinch out shoots of topiary and plants trained on structures. Pinch out growing tips on other plants, to encourage compact growth.
- Tie in long shoots before they become too woody to bend.
- Spray roses for pests and diseases.
- Prune early flowering plants just after flowering. Summer prune grape vines and wisteria.

PINCHING OUT VINES

- Continue to liquid feed container plants and any other garden plants that need it.

AUTUMN

- Bring in autumn-flowering half-hardy or tender climbers that are in containers, before the first frosts. This may extend the flowering season well into winter.
- Bring onto the verandah, or into the greenhouse, climbers in containers that are not hardy enough to withstand the winter outdoors. In warmer climates, place pots on the verandah. Choose an environment based on the plant's minimum requirements. Some need to rest. Water these plants only minimally to reduce active growth.
- Prune back climbing roses by thinning out some old growths. Some late flowering clematis may be partially cut back now, reserving harder pruning for late winter.
- Scatter winter mulches such as rotted manure on the surface of borders and beds to be dug in during the spring.
- Protect tender climbers that are to stay out over winter with hessian or straw held in place with chicken wire.
- Plant out hardy climbers while the soil is still warm and root growth still active. Plants established now withstand droughts better than those that are spring planted.

WINTER

- Continue planting out hardy plants until the first frosts.
- Check winter protection, such as straw (secured with chicken wire, to hold it in place) or hessian, around tender climbers.

STRAW

- For protection, generously mulch tuberous climbers like bomareas and *Tropaeolum speciosum*.
- Winter prune wisteria and grape vines, except when the temperature is below freezing. Remove dead wood from woody climbers.
- Use this time to investigate the supports for your climbers, such as trellis, vine eyes, and wires, to make sure that they are secure and to add any new ones where required. Remove plants entirely from their supports, if necessary, and then re-attach them.
- Treat all timber supports with horticultural preservatives that will not poison plants.

PLANTING CLIMBERS

The BEST TIME FOR PLANTING hardy climbers is autumn or early spring, whereas half-hardy plants should be planted only in spring or early summer. Before you plant, ensure you have the necessary soil conditioners to hand, such as well-rotted garden compost, manure, and fertilizers, to match each climber's needs.

PLANTING AGAINST A WALL

The soil by a wall is often dry, because it is protected from rainfall, but organic matter can improve the moisture retention of the soil as well as adding nutrients. Work in a balanced fertilizer and thoroughly water the area before planting. Plant the climber 40cm (16in) away from the base of the wall and then train it to grow towards the wall.

1 Dig the hole at least 45cm (18in) wide and deep, or three times the plant width. Mix in rotted manure or garden compost.

2 Place the plant at an angle to the wall. Use a cane across the hole to check that the top of the rootball is at ground level.

3 Fill the hole with a mixture of rotted manure or garden compost and soil, firm around the roots, and water in thoroughly.

4 Spread the stems out, and tie in to two or three canes. Mulch with rotted manure or bark to retain moisture.

WHERE TO PLANT

Structures such as wooden trellis and metal arbours may need to be treated or repaired every few years. Position climbers up to 40cm (16in) away from such structures, so that plants can be easily pulled away when maintenance work is being carried out. When growing through other trees or shrubs, position the climber outside the outer canopy of the host plant, to ensure that the plants are not competing for nutrients and water.

PLANTING UP AN ARCH
You will need to plant both sides of an arch because many climbers will not climb down the other side very well. Plant the climber 30–40cm (12–16in) away for ease of maintenance.

PROTECTING THE ROOTS

It is good practice to mulch the roots of all newly planted climbers, to help keep weeds at bay and to prevent the soil from drying out. Clematis in particular will benefit from a layer of sharp gravel to keep their roots cool and white gravel has the added benefit of helping to reflect heat. Stone slabs and bark can be used but these can often harbour pests such as slugs, snails, and earwigs, which climb the plants at night and chew the leaves, flowers, and stems.

A GRAVEL COVER
A sharp, pale gravel mulch is inhospitable to slugs. Spread to a depth of 3–5cm (1–2in), it reflects heat to keep roots both cool and moist, while also helping to keep weeds down.

TIPS ON MULCHING
• Spread mulches up to a depth of 5cm (2in).
• Special woven fabrics allow moisture through but prevent weeds from growing. Plastic or newspaper mulches may not be very attractive but they can be disguised with chipped bark.
• Mulches such as rotted manures, composts, and grass cuttings feed the plant as well as conserving moisture.
• Stones, rocks, old tiles, slates, and gravel can all be useful as mulches, but some are difficult to weed between.
• Be sure that whatever mulch you choose doesn't harbour pests that could damage or destroy the plants.

ORGANIC MULCHES

These mulches can take many forms. Chipped bark is attractive and popular but, unless composted, it can deplete the soil of nutrients as it breaks down, making additional fertilizer necessary. Some mulches, like rotted manure or garden compost, act as a fertilizer as well, although weeds may be a problem in the latter as seeds can survive the composting process.

▶ MULCH AROUND BASE
Mulching around the base of a plant up to 1m (3ft) away, or over an entire bed of plants, can look attractive, feed the plant, and prevent hardening, or capping, of the soil surface. Take care to keep the area around the plant stems clear.

SPRAYING LEAVES
• Keep newly planted seedlings fresh and turgid after the stress of planting by gently spraying with water.
• Add liquid fertilizers, such as liquid seaweed, into the spray to promote growth.
• Spray plants early in the morning before the sun is hot. Young foliage can be scorched when sprayed in hot sunshine, leading to unsightly markings on the leaves. Spray pesticides and fungicides in the early morning or evening, when bees and other beneficial insects are not around.

SPRAY YOUNG SWEET PEAS

PLANTING IN A POT

When planting climbing plants in pots, it is important to ensure that the pot is of a suitable size. It is usually better to move a plant into a pot one size bigger every year than to plant a small plant in an over large pot. Do not leave vigorous plants in pots that are too small. They will become pot-bound and not grow as well when repotted. Choose the right compost for your plant. If it is a lime-hater it will need an appropriate compost. Soilless composts dry out very quickly, so a loam-based one is preferable.

Position the tripod before adding the compost.

Half fill pot with compost, firming it around supports.

Gently reposition the growth onto the new support.

Plant, and add more compost, firming it in around the supports.

1 **Insert the support canes** and half fill the pot with potting compost, firming the canes into position. Scoop out a hole for the plant.

2 **Holding the rootball** carefully, insert the climber. Top up with compost, firm the plant into an upright position, and water thoroughly.

3 **Tease out the stems** carefully, and gently spiral the shoots around the supports. Once the stems are in position, gently tie them to the supports.

PLANTING IN A HANGING BASKET

Some climbing plants are very well suited to trailing out of hanging baskets, and they may be tucked into the underside of baskets so that they can trail downwards. Nasturtiums, black-eyed Susans, miniature climbing roses, and some clematis are all ideal. Ivy, especially small-leaved variegated forms, can be used in this way in both sun and shade.

There are different styles of basket for indoor and outdoor use, according to the methods of watering required; those for indoor use have integral drip trays or an outer container with no drainage holes. Take care not to overwater these. For outdoor use, try experimenting with large baskets with plenty of potting compost because these are less likely to dry out too quickly. It is usually necessary to replant hanging baskets each year.

Plant variegated ivy through the basket sides.

PLANT FIRMLY
The basket may need a top up of potting compost after watering. Firm the plants again and water a second time before hanging.

DISPLAYING ON A FRAME

Ivy, jasmine, *Clematis florida* varieties, and passion flowers can all be trained around frames because of their long, flexible stems. Wire frames can be bought, but it is quite easy to make your own globe or cone out of a sturdy plastic-coated wire. Bend the wire and secure it into the required shape with pieces of thinner wire or twine. You may also need a single cane to hold the globe stable while the plant becomes established.

1 Secure the wire frame in the pot by weighting it with stones. Fill the pot with potting compost and plant the climber in the centre.

2 Gently wind the stems (here, passion flower) around the wires. They will soon use their own tendrils to secure themselves to the frame.

3 Tidy up loose ends and trim off unwanted shoots. Pinch out the tips of very long shoots to encourage fresh growth. Water in thoroughly.

FORMING AN IVY PYRAMID

Ivies also make excellent subjects for training as topiary or simple shapes like cones or pyramids. For small pots, choose one of the very small-leaved varieties. Ivy withstands plenty of trimming and pinching out at almost any time of year. Frost-proof pots can be placed outside in winter, but young ivy leaves become easily browned and discoloured in cold winters. Ivy enjoys cool conditions, and too much heat will make them too dry.

WIND IVY AROUND FRAME
Weave the plant in and out of the wires as new growth develops. Pinch out shoots to encourage young basal growth.

PRACTICAL TIPS

• Choose a pot that is in proportion to the size of the plant: don't isolate plants in too large a pot.

• Plants in pots need to be fed and watered regularly. Liquid fertilizers are easy to use and foliar feeds encourage glossy leaves.

• Overgrown plants can be cut right down and their new growth retrained each spring.

• If the plant shows little or no growth, remove it from the pot and knock off some of the old compost. Replant in the same pot with fresh compost.

METHODS OF CLIMBING

THE MAJORITY OF CLIMBERS have flexible stems that twine around the twigs and branches of other plants, but others have evolved highly specialized methods of attaching themselves to their supports. Some, such as ivy, have clinging stems, by which they attach themselves to surfaces. Some have modified leaves that have evolved to become tendrils or whose leaf stalks, or petioles, can twist like tendrils. Without a host, scandent climbers would form loose shrubby mounds.

MATCHING A CLIMBER TO ITS SUPPORT

Before deciding on what kind of support to erect for a climber, make sure you know what climbing method it uses. Some may not need any support, such as those with clinging stem roots and adhesive pads. Others, like those with fine stem and leaf tendrils, need thin supports like wire, plastic mesh, twigs, or bamboo canes. Scrambling or scandent climbers in general, and those with twisting and twining stems, or hooked thorns, should be tied into supports of stout wire or wooden trellis.

PRACTICAL TIPS

• Trellis should be stout enough to support the weight of the climber when it matures. Wisteria is so strong it can break lightweight structures.

• Wires should be thick enough to support not only a branch, but also the whole plant if it reaches the top of a wall and hangs off.

• Vine eyes and nails must be firmly embedded into walls, using a masonry drill and rawlplugs where necessary.

• Plastic mesh can be unattractive in winter if used for a deciduous or annual climber, but is suitable if the plant will hide it completely.

STEM TENDRILS
These are shoots that grow out from a stem. Once they have coiled around a support, the coil tightens to draw the plant to its host (here Passiflora).

HOOKED THORNS
Thorns on bougainvillea (as here) and other scrambling plants protect the plant from animals and can be hooked to hold onto other plants.

ADHESIVE PADS
These branched, tendril-type modifications (here on parthenocissus) have touch-sensitive adhesive pads that can stick to most surfaces.

TWINING LEAF STALKS
*Young leaf stems have evolved
to twist around small twigs
and wires or even each other,
while developing into full-
grown leaves. Clematis are the
most typical.*

TWINING STEMS
*The most common method
involves plants (here Jasminum)
twisting around almost any
structure that they touch,
clockwise or anti-clockwise
depending on the species.*

CLINGING STEM ROOTS
*These (here on Hedera) cling
to virtually any surface,
except glass, and can damage
loose mortar and paintwork,
when the plant is removed.*

LEAF TENDRILS
*These modified leaves have
evolved into tendrils (here on
lathyrus). Like true tendrils,
they have a coiled spring to
draw themselves to a support.*

PLANT LIST

STEM TENDRILS
*Ampelopsis, Cissus
Passiflora, Vitis*

**SCRAMBLING
(SCANDENT)**
*Bomarea, Bougainvillea
Celastrus, Clianthus
Jasminum, Plumbago
Rosa, Rubus
Solanum*

ADHESIVE PADS
Cissus, Parthenocissus

**TWINING
LEAF STALKS**
*Clematis, Rhodochiton
Tropaeolum*

LOOSELY TWINING
*Berberidopsis
Billardiera
Cucurbita, Lapageria
Muehlenbeckia*

STRONGLY TWINING
*Actinidia, Akebia
Aristolochia
Campsis, Celastrus
Dregea, Fallopia
Gelsemium, Holboellia
Humulus, Ipomoea
Jasminum, Lonicera
Schisandra, Sollya
Thunbergia
Trachelospermum
Tweedia, Wisteria*

**CLINGING STEM
ROOTS**
*Campsis, Cucurbita
Euonymus, Ficus,
Hedera
Hydrangea anomola* subsp.
 *petiolaris
Pileostegia
Schizophragma*

LEAF TENDRILS
*Bignonia, Cobaea
Dicentra
Eccremocarpus
Lathyrus*

PUTTING UP SUPPORTS

MOST SUPPORTS FOR CLIMBING PLANTS can be erected simply and easily with a hammer, screwdriver, drill, and a ladder. Make sure that the materials chosen are strong enough and the surfaces are sturdy and firm enough to take screws and nails. Particular care must be taken when erecting supports on tall buildings from a ladder. In such cases, it may be better to hire suitable safety equipment or use the services of a professional.

EQUIPMENT

The simplest equipment comprises nails or staples and lightweight plastic-coated wire, especially on wooden fences. Vine eyes are recommended for stone and brick walls and holes should be drilled and rawlplugs used to secure them. Some are designed to be hammered into soft mortar. Wire or plastic netting can be used, but plants often become deeply entangled in them, making it hard to tidy up. Netting and trellis should be mounted on battens, to give the plant the space to twist behind the support.

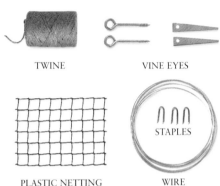

TWINE

VINE EYES

PLASTIC NETTING

STAPLES

WIRE

PUTTING UP NETTING
Wide-meshed netting is less obtrusive and easy to attach to wooden fences.

USING VINE EYES
Set up a grid of vine eyes and stretch wire along them, ensuring that it is tight.

WOODEN TRELLIS

• Trellis may be up for many years and should be strong enough to support a mature plant so make it out of strong laths.

• Nail 5cm (2in) battens to the wall and fix the trellis to the battens. This will leave space for the plants to grow behind the trellis and make it easier to repaint the trellis at a later date. Attach the trellis with hooks and hinges to make it less difficult to remove for maintenance.

• Trellis can be designed to be a beautiful feature in its own right, incorporating *trompe l'oeil* effects and mirrors.

• Freestanding trellis should be secured strongly at its base, since when the plant is full grown, winds can blow against it like a sail.

USING WOOD STAIN
Softwood trellis needs preserving with wood stain. Hardwoods, teak, cedar, and redwood benefit from being oiled every few years.

MAKING A WIGWAM SUPPORT

Wigwam supports are particularly good for annual lightweight climbers like sweet peas (*Lathyrus*) and late-flowering clematis. They can be made of bamboo canes or rustic poles, held together by twine or wire. More wire or twine is then spiralled around them. It is possible to buy ready-made willow or bamboo wigwams in a variety of beautiful shapes.

2 Weave in and out of the canes to make the wigwam as wide or as narrow as you wish.

1 Tie 12 or more willow canes together at the top with some twine or wire. Intertwine 3 or 4 lengths of willow together and weave them in a spiral.

3 Tie off the ends with twine. Leave enough cane at the base to press into the ground.

GROWING OVER ARCHES

An arch is an excellent feature to place over a garden gate or to act as a transition from one part of the garden to another. Choose an arch that is wider than your path to allow for plant growth on the inside. Arches can be bought in timber, wrought iron, or plastic-coated tubular metal. They can also be made using willow poles or freshly cut bamboo canes. Heavy duty plastic, copper, or steel tubing can be bent to make an arch too. Long twigs of freshly cut willow pushed into the ground may root and grow to make a living arch. When choosing climbers to cover an arch, make sure that they are compatible for pruning and that they are not going to be too vigorous. Remember when using roses that their growth is thorny.

RUSTIC ARCH
Prunings of whippy plants like willow and bamboo can be woven and bent into an arch to make a structure for lightweight climbers.

GENERAL PRUNING

T HE REASON FOR PRUNING CLIMBERS is to create a well-balanced, healthy plant that flowers well. Some may never need any pruning when they have climbed high up into trees or other inaccessible places, or they may naturally fit their space well and require little attention. Often, however, plants grow too large or tall, and so need to be cut down, or others start to become unproductive and so need their old wood cut out to generate new growth.

ROUTINE TASKS

Pruning to encourage flowering and good health is usually carried out once or twice a year, and needs to be timed to fit the flowering time and habit of the plant. In general, climbers that flower in spring need to be pruned immediately after flowering, while summer-flowering ones can be pruned in the spring before growth starts. Pruning for shape should be done in winter (after leaf fall) for deciduous climbers and in spring for evergreens.

Use clean, sharp secateurs for pruning. Plants that produce thin, tangled growth can be pruned with shears, while thick, old wood may need to be pruned with lopping shears or a pruning saw. Feed and mulch the plant well after pruning.

ALTERNATE BUDS
Prune stems with alternate buds, with an angled cut. The top of the cut should be just above a bud and the base of the cut should not touch the bud.

OPPOSITE BUDS
Prune stems with buds opposite each other straight across, just above the buds. A snag can cause growth to die back and may encourage disease.

REPLACEMENT SHOOT
To encourage a new shoot to take over, prune to a vigorous shoot that is pointing in the direction you want it to climb. Cut above the leaf junction.

DEAD WOOD
Dead wood or frost damage may not show until spring. If there is no sign of new healthy buds, prune out the dead growth down to the live shoots.

DEADHEAD
Some plants benefit from having old flowering shoots removed, to help stimulate further flowers and new growth (here bougainvillea).

PRUNING ESTABLISHED CLIMBERS

Regular pruning of an established climber will keep it healthy and stimulate good flowering or fruiting. Plants need to be carefully examined to make sure that there is plenty of air circulating within its framework to discourage diseases, that any weak or twiggy growth is removed, and that a well-branched habit is developing. Pruning out whole shoots will encourage new ones from the base, but too much pruning may overstimulate the plant, promoting leafy growth at the expense of flowers.

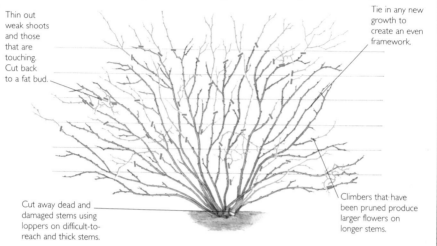

Thin out weak shoots and those that are touching. Cut back to a fat bud.

Tie in any new growth to create an even framework.

Cut away dead and damaged stems using loppers on difficult-to-reach and thick stems.

Climbers that have been pruned produce larger flowers on longer stems.

RENOVATING ESTABLISHED CLIMBERS

Climbers that have become overgrown and neglected are often top heavy, full of dead twigs and wood, and are less profuse in their flowering. In cases where there is more dead wood than live growth, it may be better to dig up the plant and replace it with a young vigorous one. Otherwise, renovation is best done in the winter or very early spring, having carefully removed the plant from its supports.

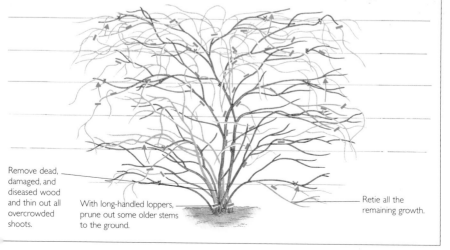

Remove dead, damaged, and diseased wood and thin out all overcrowded shoots.

With long-handled loppers, prune out some older stems to the ground.

Retie all the remaining growth.

PRUNING WISTERIA AND GRAPE VINES

WISTERIA AND GRAPE VINES need very similar pruning because both plants share the habit of building up flowering, and therefore fruiting, spurs. Spurs are tight bunches of flower buds borne close to the main stems of the plant. The secret of success with such climbers is to carry out the pruning twice a year in order to maximize flower output. The same method can be applied to apple and pear trees, and greatly increases productivity.

WHEN AND HOW TO PRUNE WISTERIA

If you have a young plant that is five or six years old, the first priority is to form a good structure, especially if it is grown on a house wall, where you need good strong branches. These growths will carry all the spurs, so it is important that they are well placed and secure. Wisterias should start flowering at about seven or eight years old.

Prune first in summer, shortening the long whippy growths back by two-thirds of their lengths. Then in midwinter, but not while it

is frosty, shorten these stems again, down to two or three buds. This is the beginning of the spur building. Pruning only once a year will simply encourage a lot of whippy growth and produce few flowers.

An older, well-pruned specimen, flowering in spring, will flower without too much foliage hiding the evenly distributed blooms, and its structure of twisted vines will look all the more handsome during the winter months.

PRUNING AND TRAINING
In summer, tie in shoots that will form the basic structure and secure them well. Remove all superfluous growth. Two months after flowering, shorten the long growths by two-thirds to within five or six buds of a main branch.

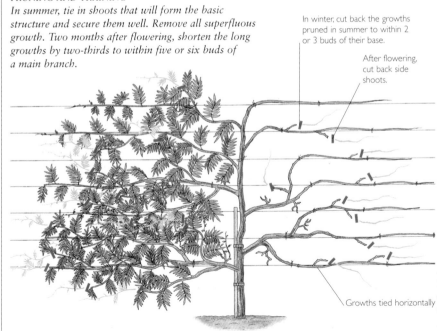

In winter, cut back the growths pruned in summer to within 2 or 3 buds of their base.

After flowering, cut back side shoots.

Growths tied horizontally

PRUNING GRAPE VINES

The majority of grape vines respond to a similar pruning regime as wisteria, with a twice yearly pruning. The system shown below is the rod and spur system, and many other climbers can be pruned in this manner, whether small plants grown against a wall or wire fence, or large plants grown over a pergola. Winter pruning must be done when the vine is resting in midwinter, since, later on, the shoots bleed sap when cut.

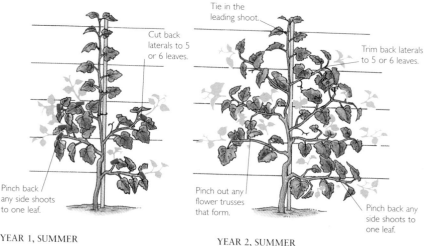

Cut back laterals to 5 or 6 leaves.

Pinch back any side shoots to one leaf.

Tie in the leading shoot.

Trim back laterals to 5 or 6 leaves.

Pinch out any flower trusses that form.

Pinch back any side shoots to one leaf.

YEAR 1, SUMMER
Having trained a single main shoot, or shoots if training over a pergola, the process of building a spur system can begin.

YEAR 2, SUMMER
While still building the structure of the vine, it is best to remove all flowers and fruits, which can spoil the shape and drain the plant's energy.

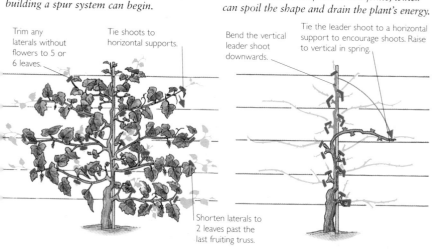

Trim any laterals without flowers to 5 or 6 leaves.

Tie shoots to horizontal supports.

Bend the vertical leader shoot downwards.

Tie the leader shoot to a horizontal support to encourage shoots. Raise to vertical in spring.

Shorten laterals to 2 leaves past the last fruiting truss.

ESTABLISHED, SUMMER
Summer pruning of established vines involves thinning out and shortening all sideshoots, to help build spurs and to ensure that fruits are not too shaded or crowded.

ESTABLISHED, WINTER
All laterals should be pruned back to one or two buds; if buds are congested, thin them out. Pruning must be done in midwinter, because, later on, vines bleed when cut.

PRUNING ROSES

MANY CLIMBING ROSES ARE CLIMBING FORMS of bush roses. None of them strictly climbs, and long whippy stems need to be tied in if grown against a wall. The vigorous long growths of rambling roses can be tricky to train on a wall around windows and doors, but they can be effectively grown through trees and left untended for many years. In general, all of these need some pruning from time to time and, for a healthy plant, this should be every year.

WHEN AND HOW TO PRUNE ROSES

Many climbing roses are repeat flowering, while most ramblers flower only once. Pruning can be carried out in autumn, but in cold regions this can be delayed to early spring just before the buds start expanding. The reason for this is that some roses may experience winter damage, and leaving on the old wood protects the dormant buds lower down the plant. If these stems are pruned too hard in autumn, the buds may be stimulated and damaged. Pruning in midsummer may stimulate young growth that is too soft to withstand the rigours of winter. Pruning too late in the spring, after bud break, will delay flowering, although further pruning can be carried out after the first flush to encourage later flowers and new growth.

Cut just above a bud, sloping the secateurs away from it.

A GOOD CUT
A good clean cut is important because rose shoots are very prone to die-back.

RENEWAL PRUNING
The old stems of a rose are gradually removed to stimulate new growth. Prune close to where branches break from the main stems. Look for strong buds or shoots and prune above them. For pruning small branches, use sharp secateurs or loppers, but for thick trunks, it is better to use a pruning saw.

Use loppers to cut out old wood very close to a young stem.

PRACTICAL TIPS

• Use only sharp tools to achieve clean cuts because blunt blades bruise rose wood easily, encouraging disease.
• Don't leave snags below the pruning cuts.
• Prune in autumn or winter in mild areas.
• Prune in spring in cold regions.
• Pruning after buds break delays flowering.
• Deadhead roses to prolong flowering, especially climbers.
• Stop deadheading after midsummer to prevent stimulation of late, frost-prone growth.

• Feed roses well after pruning, especially adding rotted manure as a mulch over the roots area.
• Diseased foliage and wood should be burnt or otherwise disposed of.
• Keep the ground under roses clear of fallen leaves in autumn in order to discourage unsightly black spot and other diseases.
• Look out for suckers, which usually shoot from below the ground, and try to pull them off. These grow from the vigorous rootstock and will weaken the main plant if allowed to grow.

WALL-TRAINED CLIMBING ROSES

Wall-trained roses need frequent renewal because they tend to have quite leggy growth, with flowers being produced high on the plant. This calls for replacement shoots to be promoted from near the base of the plant. New long shoots, if trained horizontally, will flower more readily, especially if the shoots are tip pruned.

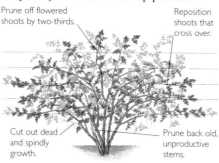

Remove dead and diseased shoots.

Tip prune non-branching shoots.

Prune off flowered shoots by two-thirds.

Reposition shoots that cross over.

Tie in new growth, spreading shoots out wide.

Canes tied to shoots guide stems to wall.

Cut out dead and spindly growth.

Prune back old, unproductive stems.

YEAR 1, SUMMER
Summer pruning involves tip pruning shoots to promote branching and also spreading out shoots to create a balanced framework.

ESTABLISHED, AUTUMN
Established climbers need frequent renewal, because old shoots become unproductive after 3–4 years. New shoots need space and tying in.

ESTABLISHED RAMBLERS

Rambling roses have one flush of flowers in summer. They have more flexible stems than climbers and can be bent and twisted into special effects (*see p.53*). In a wild garden they will need no pruning, but in more confined spaces, old stems can be pruned after flowering to make way for the growth that will carry next year's blooms.

PRUNING RAMBLERS
- Prune after flowering in early to midsummer.
- Remove old flowering shoots.
- Train or tie in new long, whippy shoots.
- Shorten sideshoots to encourage flowering.
- Bend, peg down, or spiral the shoots.
- Feed ramblers well if hard pruning.

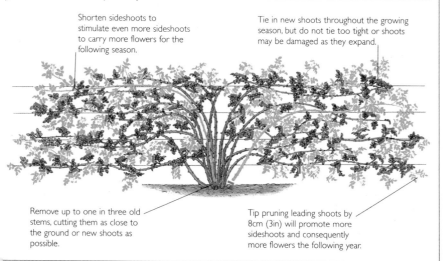

Shorten sideshoots to stimulate even more sideshoots to carry more flowers for the following season.

Tie in new shoots throughout the growing season, but do not tie too tight or shoots may be damaged as they expand.

Remove up to one in three old stems, cutting them as close to the ground or new shoots as possible.

Tip pruning leading shoots by 8cm (3in) will promote more sideshoots and consequently more flowers the following year.

PRUNING CLEMATIS

THE PRUNING OF CLEMATIS need not seem daunting just because the plants are divided into three pruning groups, which relate to their different flowering times. Group 1 consists of all those species and their varieties that produce their flowers in early spring; Group 2 comprises the large-flowered hybrids that flower in early summer and sometimes again in late summer; and Group 3 describes the late flowering species and hybrids.

WHEN TO PRUNE

Pruning should be carried out at the following times. Group 1, which needs little pruning, should be pruned immediately after flowering to stimulate renewed growth. Group 2 is best left to early spring when the new buds are beginning to swell. Group 3 can be hard pruned at almost any time during the winter and early spring, but some may also be part pruned in late winter down to new shoots as they emerge.

TWICE-FLOWERING CLEMATIS, GROUP 2
This group includes all the large-flowered doubles and singles that flower in early summer and sometimes again later. They must be pruned lightly in spring.

HOW TO PRUNE

Group 1 Prune after flowering only if plants become overgrown. *C. montana* should be hard pruned with caution because thick branches sometimes do not regenerate.

Group 2 Look for large fat buds, which are the flowering shoots. Thin out old growth and last year's flowering shoots down to the fat buds, and retrain these to a prominent position.

Group 3 Prune hard to within 15–30cm (6–12in) of the ground, but some may be left alone then pruned in spring to the new shoots as they emerge from the lower parts of the plant, removing old flowering stems.

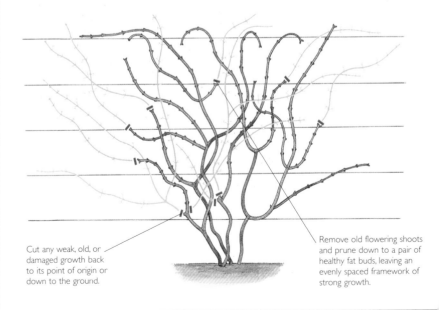

Cut any weak, old, or damaged growth back to its point of origin or down to the ground.

Remove old flowering shoots and prune down to a pair of healthy fat buds, leaving an evenly spaced framework of strong growth.

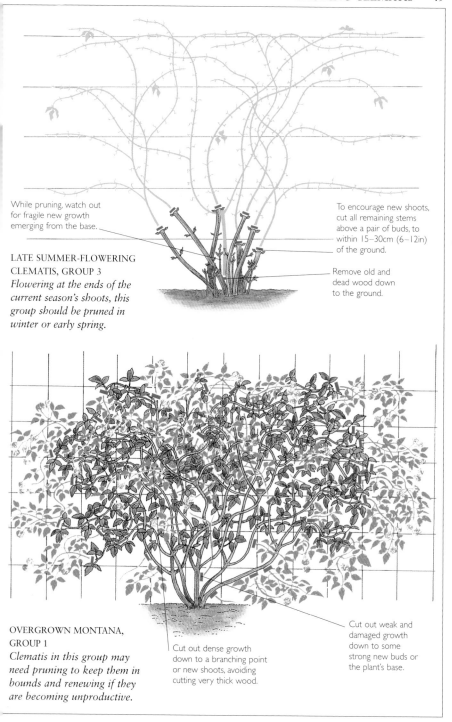

While pruning, watch out for fragile new growth emerging from the base.

To encourage new shoots, cut all remaining stems above a pair of buds, to within 15–30cm (6–12in) of the ground.

LATE SUMMER-FLOWERING CLEMATIS, GROUP 3
Flowering at the ends of the current season's shoots, this group should be pruned in winter or early spring.

Remove old and dead wood down to the ground.

OVERGROWN MONTANA, GROUP 1
Clematis in this group may need pruning to keep them in bounds and renewing if they are becoming unproductive.

Cut out dense growth down to a branching point or new shoots, avoiding cutting very thick wood.

Cut out weak and damaged growth down to some strong new buds or the plant's base.

TRAINING AND TYING

WHETHER THE PLANT IS AN ANNUAL, HERBACEOUS CLIMBER, or a woody perennial, the training and tying in of the young shoots at an early stage is important for forming a manageable structure. Some climbers can quickly become entangled with themselves or other plants and structures, while horizontally trained climbers produce more flowers and fruits than vertically grown ones. Use supports and ties that suit the climber and are strong enough for a mature plant.

TRAINING ON AN OBELISK

An obelisk can be designed to be covered by two climbers. Although it can be complicated training two plants with differing pruning methods, superb effects can be achieved.

Each plant needs different treatment. Woody climbers should be encouraged to grow horizontally, while herbaceous climbers grow more vertically and then cascade down.

1 Obelisk training Plant passion flowers at the corners and tie in their laterals. Plant *Clematis viticella* in the centre and guide the plant towards the top with strings.

2 In full flower The passion flowers will have developed fully before the clematis has reached the top, which means that it will not suffer from having too much shade.

3 Early spring Prune the passion flowers back to the laterals. Hard prune the clematis to 30cm (12in) from the ground, pulling out the old growth.

CLIMBERS ON HEDGES

• Honeysuckles can be planted with evergreens, often flowering before the hedge needs cutting.
• Clematis fill and adorn large hedges, but many flower late and may hinder hedge trimming.
• Try *Clematis macropetala* for early flowers, *C. viticella* for late and *C. vitalba* for large hedges.
• Rambling roses can be trained along a hedge, almost becoming a hedge in their own right.

• Ivy, although useful as an evergreen, may swamp other shrubby plants but is suitable with deciduous hedges like hawthorn (*Crataegus*).
• Annual climbers like morning glory will need a good start if they are to compete with the hedge for water, light, and nutrients.
• Try almost any climber or combinations of climbers, bearing in mind timing of flowering.

TRAINING ON A PERGOLA

A pergola consists of a series of pillars or posts linked together by wires or cross-beams. Pergolas are sometimes used as walkways but are more often constructed with overhead beams close to a house in order to provide shade in the summer. Climbers are then planted a short distance from the base of each pillar, some trained to clothe the pillar base while others grow over the top to form a canopy of shade.

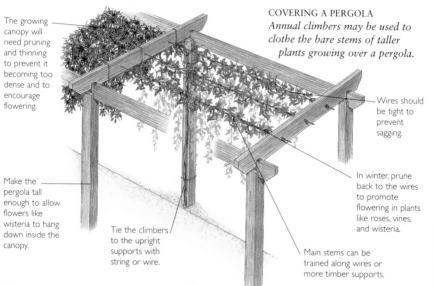

COVERING A PERGOLA
Annual climbers may be used to clothe the bare stems of taller plants growing over a pergola.

The growing canopy will need pruning and thinning to prevent it becoming too dense and to encourage flowering.

Wires should be tight to prevent sagging.

Make the pergola tall enough to allow flowers like wisteria to hang down inside the canopy.

Tie the climbers to the upright supports with string or wire.

In winter, prune back to the wires to promote flowering in plants like roses, vines, and wisteria.

Main stems can be trained along wires or more timber supports.

TYING IN

There are many materials for tying in plants: treated twine, plastic- and paper-coated wire ties, raffia, and strong rubber tree ties. For long-term plants use ties that can be loosened, since overtight wires can strangle stems as they grow and expand. On annual climbers, where the whole plant will be composted, use biodegradable materials.

1 **Direct the climber** towards the frame with an angled bamboo cane. Remove all the supporting ties attached by the nursery.

2 **Spread the plant** out evenly, using temporary ties, and ensuring that they are loose enough for the stems to grow and expand.

3 **When using twine,** form a figure of eight to buffer the stem from rubbing on the main frame. Do not twist the twine too tightly around the stem.

TRAINING AS A STANDARD

Climbers grown as standards can be an arresting sight, creating drama when planted in a border or standing alone in a sea of gravel. Wisteria, in particular, can give the appearance of a twisted small tree. Most of them will need some form of support, so the stake used for the main trunk should be durable, such as treated softwood, hardwood, or wrought iron. Frames can be mounted on these stakes. There are special umbrella frames used for weeping standard roses, but for smaller standards an upturned hanging basket may be all that is needed. More elaborate or stronger frames can be custom made. Plants that respond to spur pruning are the best choice, but avoid wiry, spindly, and tendrilled climbers, which may form an unmanageable mass.

CLIMBERS FOR STANDARDS

Actinidia kolomikta
Bignonia capreolata
Bougainvillea glabra
Campsis radicans
Hedera helix
  (many)
Hydrangea anomola
  subsp. petiolaris
Hydrangea
  seemannii
Jasminum
  polyanthum
Lonicera japonica
Lonicera
  periclymenum

Pileostegia
  viburnoides
Plumbago
  auriculata
Schizophragma
  hydrangeoides
Solanum crispum
Solanum laxum
Trachelospermum
  jasminoides
Vitis vinifera
Wisteria floribunda
Wisteria sinensis

Shorten the leading shoot in the summer by two-thirds above the top of the support.

Cut back all the laterals to 2 or 3 buds. This is known as spur pruning.

Shorten the new leader again in winter to one-third of the previously shortened growth.

YEAR 1, WINTER

Pinch out the leader at the desired height.

Shorten all the laterals by up to a half, to encourage sideshoots.

Loosen any ties where necessary.

YEAR 2, SUMMER

Shorten all new shoots by half to two-thirds for a dense head.

Remove lateral shoots from the main stem, cutting cleanly, close to the stem.

YEAR 3, SUMMER

SPIRAL TRAINING

The training of certain climbers by spiralling their growth around a structure such as a pyramid, obelisk, or post helps to keep a tall plant at a lower height. It also encourages the plant to flower, because shoots in a more horizontal position tend to flower better along their entire length than vertical shoots, which may produce flowers only at the top of their growth. Rambling and climbing roses with flexible growth, such as 'New Dawn', are the best plants for this kind of training. Roses, which normally reach heights of up to 10m (30ft), can be contained on structures as low as 3m (10ft) when spiral trained. Most other climbers, such as honeysuckle and jasmine, also respond well to spiralling.

PRACTICAL TIPS

• The operation is best carried out in winter, when almost all growth will need to be detached from the structure.
• Prune out all unproductive and diseased wood, looking out for long, whippy stems produced in the previous growing season.
• Young stems are very pliable, which makes them easy to train by tying them onto each other or the structure.

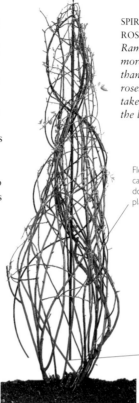

SPIRAL TRAINING ROSES
Rambling roses have more flexible stems than most climbing roses, so care must be taken when bending the latter.

Flowers will be carried low down on the plant.

Thin out all old flowering shoots over 3 years old, cutting close to the base or at the joints of new shoots.

TRANSFORMING A POST OR STUMP

Old gate posts and tree stumps make beautiful informal structures to drape with all kinds of climbers. Before cutting down old trees, especially old but healthy apple and pear trees, think of leaving a large part of the tree as a sculpted structure, removing only small branches that might be dangerous if they were to break easily and fall. Groups of mature trees can have climbers looped gracefully between them using wires for support.

OLD TREE STUMP
Covering an old stump with ivy can create a dense mass of evergreen faster than growing a small tree from scratch.

DRAPING PLANTS

Akebia quinata
Aristolochia
Campsis
Celastrus
Cissus striata
Fallopia
Ficus pumila
Hedera (most)
Humulus lupulus 'Aureus'
Hydrangea anomala subsp. *petiolaris*
Lonicera
Parthenocissus
Pileostegia viburnoides
Rosa (ramblers)
Schizophragma hydrangeoides
Vitis

INCREASING YOUR PLANTS

MANY CLIMBING PLANTS, BOTH ANNUAL and perennial, are very easy to propagate with only a minimum of equipment. Working from seed and cuttings, all that is needed is a sunny windowsill or a greenhouse, although both may be done directly in the garden. Layering is a simple way of propagating climbers, especially those with aerial roots. The latter may produce spontaneous layers that can simply be dug up and moved to a new position.

GROWING FROM SEED

Sow the seeds directly into a small seed tray or pot, covering them with a thin layer of sharp sand. When the seedlings have got at least two pairs of leaves, carefully move them into small pots and grow on until the roots fill the pots. Wait until all danger of frosts has receded and then plant them outdoors.

WELL-SPACED NASTURTIUM SEEDLINGS
Do not sow seed too thickly since overcrowded seedlings are weak and prone to disease. Seedlings can then develop well before being moved into individual small pots.

PLANTING OUT SEEDLINGS

Young plants should be handled with great care. The stem tips are often very soft and succulent and can bruise and break easily. Since they have been grown in a protected environment, they are more prone to wilting and sun-scorch if planted out in the middle of the day. Plant in the evening, water well and, if necessary, shelter them with shade netting from drying winds and protect them from the full sun until they are settled in.

1 Planting out a young plant. Work plenty of rotted organic matter in the planting hole, hold the plant in position, and firm the earth around the roots carefully. Water in thoroughly.

2 Support the plant. Push a cane in, taking care not to damage the roots, and tie the shoots to it with soft twine. Protect the young plant from winds and bright sun for a few days.

LAYERING AND CUTTING

The easiest way to produce one or two new plants is by simple layering. If this isn't possible, rooting cuttings of some species can be relatively easy. Such methods ensure the new plant exactly resembles its parent, which is essential for growing hybrids that tend not to come true from seed. The simplest cuttings to take are hardwood ones; do these in autumn and plunge them into some well-cultivated ground in the shade.

LAYERING TIPS

- Choose young, healthy shoots to layer, as they are the most flexible.
- The best time to layer is in spring or autumn.
- A number of plants, such as honeysuckle and ivy, can be layered without scoring the stem or using rooting hormone.
- Mulch the area around the layered shoot and water in dry periods.

1 Layering a clematis. Choose a long healthy stem that easily bends to the ground. Where the bent stem touches the soil, score it with a knife on a clear area between leaf junctions.

2 Dip the scored area into some hormone rooting powder or liquid and shake off any excess. This will encourage the damaged area to produce its own roots.

3 Bury a pot filled with moist compost and push the treated area of the stem gently into it, holding it in place with a bent wire. You can also bury it directly into the soil.

Gently tie the stem to a cane.

4 The shoot tip can then be trained upwards and tied to a cane. The scored area should have rooted in 12–18 months, when it can be severed from the parent plant.

RECOMMENDED CLIMBING PLANTS

CHOOSING PLANTS

THIS SECTION OF THE BOOK offers a catalogue of some of the most attractive climbing plants. When you are choosing a plant, there are many factors that you need to be aware of. First and foremost, you must consider the degree of hardiness of a plant, its suitability to your climate, and your garden's situation. Other factors such as soil type and moisture levels can be adjusted (although only to a certain extent) through the use of soil additives and irrigation.

KEY TO SYMBOLS
In this catalogue each plant has been coded with a box to indicate its method of climbing.

It is important to bear in mind the method of climbing when considering the type of supports your chosen plants require.

 Scrambling (scandent)

 Loosely twining

 Strongly twining

 Twining leaf stalks

 Stem tendrils

 Leaf tendrils

 Clinging stem roots

 Adhesive pads

PLANT CHARACTERISTICS

Having chosen a plant that will survive in your garden, you need to consider what aspect it prefers (sunny or shady conditions), its ultimate height, the method by which it climbs, whether it will need to be tied in, or if it will be self-supporting. Make sure that the plant will not damage the surface of a building, block gutters, or be too strong for the trellis or wires that you have in mind.

Finally, having narrowed down the choice, the fun can begin of selecting a plant for the colour of its flowers, the time of year that it blooms, for its evergreen foliage, or beautiful fragrance.

SWEET PEAS
Grown as annuals, sweet peas (Lathyrus) can be planted for picking as cut flowers. They keep producing flowers all summer.

CLIMBING HYDRANGEA *A beautiful plant for a garden or house wall.*

ACTINIDIA

Frost hardy *Actinidia deliciosa*, also known as Chinese gooseberry or kiwi fruit, is a vigorous, deciduous, twisting climber. The leaves and stems are hairy and often tinged red. The creamy-white flowers turn yellow in summer. In warmer climates, the ovoid, bristly skinned, olive-green fruits ripen to brown in late summer. Although it quite readily produces fruit when male and female plants are close together, kiwis are often grown purely for their foliage. *A. kolomikta* ♀ is a fully hardy climber that can reach 7m (22ft) in height. It has heart-shaped to ovate leaves. Purplish when young, these turn a metallic green before becoming suffused with pink and white, near the tips of the leaves. To ensure good colouring (which may take a few years to show), plant in full sun with wires for support. The small, white flowers are slightly fragrant. Prune in late winter or early spring.

AKEBIA

A semi-evergreen twiner, *Akebia quinata,* or chocolate vine, is fairly vigorous and fully hardy. It is easily grown against a wall or on a trellis, where it will often layer itself along the base and spread freely. The leaves are shiny, with five leaflets to a stalk (three in the similar species *A. trifoliata*). Thriving best on acid or loamy soils, this climber is capable of reaching 12m (40ft). The small flowers, produced in early spring, are dusky purple, pendulous, and often in small clusters. They may be partly hidden by foliage, but carry a pervasive fragrance. The greyish-violet, sausage-shaped fruits are produced only in hot summers and when plants from different clones are present. Chocolate vines are best planted in full sun. They twine around wires or other plants. Be careful not to let chocolate vines overwhelm less vigorous plants around them. Prune in late spring, after flowering.

AMPELOPSIS

Ampelopsis glandulosa var. *brevipedunculata* is an attractive, hardy, vigorous, deciduous vine that can grow up to 10m (30ft). Its three-lobed, coarsely toothed leaves (like those of a hop) turn bright yellow in autumn. The chief attraction of this plant is the colour of its autumn fruits, which are dark porcelain-blue with purplish tints. The fruits are produced freely after a hot summer or when planted against a warm wall, and are all the more conspicuous when the leaves have fallen. Ampelopsis are easily grown in most soil types. The leaves of *A. glandulosa* 'Elegans' are splashed pink and white. Its young shoots are pink. A magnificent foliage plant, *A. megalophylla* has doubly pinnate leaves up to 40cm (16in) long. It has black fruits and, in a sunny position, good autumn tints. Ampelopsis may be left to scramble at will or, if grown on house walls, can be pruned hard in midwinter.

ACTINIDIA KOLOMIKTA ♀

AKEBIA QUINATA

AMPELOPSIS GLANDULOSA VAR. *BREVIPEDUNCULATA*

ARISTOLOCHIA

Commonly known as Dutchman's pipe, *Aristolochia macrophylla* is a frost hardy, deciduous, woody perennial with large, heart-shaped leaves. The yellowish-green flowers are long, drooping tubes that turn upwards like a smoker's pipe or a tiny saxophone. They are purplish-brown inside. The shape of the flower traps insects, which then pollinate the plant. Flowers appear in early to midsummer but are often hidden among the foliage. Easily grown in sun or shade and in most soil types, the plant enjoys a peaty loam best, with good moisture retention. It is quite a vigorous climber, reaching 5–10m (15–30ft), and can be grown up trees, over stumps, or on a trellis or arch. For dramatic effect it can be grown up a pole, making a column of greenery. Other species are less hardy, but all carry the same characteristic flower shape. Prune in late winter or early spring.

BERBERIDOPSIS

Berberidopsis corallina is an unusual and beautiful evergreen, twining climber from Chile. It grows 3–4m (10–12ft) tall, and is hardy down to –10°C (14°F). It has leathery, dark green leaves, which are white on the underside. Its stems are only very loosely twining, so it must either be given plenty of wires for support or be encouraged to scramble through a large shrub. The drooping clusters of small, globular, brilliant crimson flowers are produced in mid- to late summer and, when seen from a distance, seem to resemble berries. The contrast between the dark leaves and the red flowers is particularly striking. Berberidopsis are acid-loving plants, preferring moist soils that have been enriched with leaf mould or organic matter. In some gardens they will need protection from cold winds, but they can be planted against a shady wall. Prune in early spring when necessary.

BIGNONIA

Native to south-eastern parts of the USA, *Bignonia capreolata* is a frost hardy, evergreen climber, with lustrous leaves. Known as the cross vine, it is rapid in growth, and in mild Mediterranean climates is capable of covering the side of a house. It makes a superb conservatory plant in colder climates. The flowers are trumpet-shaped and form in clusters in the leaf junctions, sometimes almost smothering the plant in early summer. The flowers are orange-peach in colour, streaked yellow inside, but there are red-purple forms. Cross vines cling to supports by tendrils that emerge from the end of each leaf stalk. It is therefore best to provide a trellis or wires to help them climb. Cross vines grow in almost any soil type but particularly enjoy acid soils. They need plenty of sun to flower well. In cold winters they may lose their leaves. Prune after flowering or in early spring.

ARISTOLOCHIA MACROPHYLLA

BERBERIDOPSIS CORALLINA

BIGNONIA CAPREOLATA

BILLARDIERA

A small, slender twining climber, **Billardiera longiflora** ♀ is an evergreen from Australia and is frost hardy. The leaves are quite small and dark green, while the nodding flowers – tubular with a flared mouth – are lime-green with a tracery of small, black lines. The flowers on them are followed in late summer by a dramatic display of small, metallic violet-blue berries (the colour can vary in the wild). '**Cherry Berry**', has red fruits, while '**Fructo-albo**' has pure white fruits, larger than those of the species. Both are less vigorous than the species, which grows to about 3m (10ft). Billardieras require plenty of sun and prefer any reasonably fertile soil. Because they can be prone to stem rot, the soil should be very well-drained and remain dry during the winter. Billardieras are ideal subjects for a conservatory. Prune in early spring or late summer after the fruits.

BOMAREA

Bomarea caldasii ♀ is a herbaceous, twining plant, which dies down to a fleshy, tuberous rootstock each year. It comes from South America and is closely related to *Alstroemeria*. Bomareas have soft and succulent stems with lance-shaped leaves that thrust upwards until they reach a suitable host. *B. caldasii* has bunches of long, narrow, tubular, reddish-orange flowers with distinct markings inside. It flowers from midsummer until the autumn, when it produces interesting seedheads. Bomareas are easily grown from seed and, although half hardy, if they are planted in a sunny position next to a warm house wall with the rootstock protected, they may be able to stand air temperatures that drop below freezing. There are several other *Bomarea* species and hybrids available, featuring a wide range of flower colours including green, red, pink, and yellow. Prune in spring.

BOUGAINVILLEA

This is a popular evergreen climber in warm climates. It prefers to stay above 10°C (50°F) but in colder and less sunny areas the purple-magenta (the natural colour for **Bougainvillea glabra** ♀) is the easiest and toughest form to try. The many other forms available vary from white to salmon pink. The small flowers are carried throughout summer along the main shoots, surrounded by persistent, brightly coloured, papery bracts. Bougainvilleas can, therefore, give the impression of "flowering" for a long time. They may be container-grown, but they must be fed well and, because they resent root disturbance, care must be taken when potting on. For best flowering performance in a conservatory, keep the temperature high. In some frost-prone areas, it is just possible to grow them outside, but they must be kept fairly dry in winter. Prune in late winter or early spring.

BILLARDIERA LONGIFLORA ♀

BOMAREA CALDASII ♀

BOUGAINVILLEA GLABRA ♀

CAMPSIS

Campsis × *tagliabuana* 'Madame Galen' ♀, the trumpet vine, is a hybrid between two species found in the USA and China. It is deciduous and frost hardy, but it needs plenty of sun to produce the large, drooping clusters of orange-red to apricot, trumpet-shaped flowers in late summer. The large leaves have oval, toothed leaflets. Trumpet vine is partly self-clinging but often needs extra support on a wall. It also climbs by twining around host plants or wires. Trumpet vine may reach 10m (30ft) or more, with new shoots 3m (10ft) long. It can be kept in check by being planted in poor soil, and can be pruned in early spring to within a few buds of the old wood. In frost-prone areas trumpet vine should be planted against a sunny wall. Other species are *C. grandiflora* and the hardier *C. radicans* whose form *flava* ♀ has yellow trumpets.

CELASTRUS

A strong-growing, deciduous climber up to 15m (50ft) tall, *Celastrus orbiculatus* is also known as oriental bittersweet. It is aided in its twining by small spines on the young shoots. The plant is spectacular in autumn, when the leaves turn yellow then drop, revealing hundreds of scarlet, pea-sized fruits held in half-opened golden-yellow capsules. If plants of both sexes are present or if a good hermaphrodite selection is grown, these cover the vine. They may stay well into winter – when bittersweet is cut for decoration. The Chinese *C. orbiculatus* and the American native *C. scandens* (American bittersweet) are both fully hardy, but the former fruits more readily in less sunny regions. Bittersweet is best grown up an old tree where it can climb right through and cascade out of its host. Prune in winter or early spring.

CISSUS

Belonging to a large family of mostly tropical climbers, some of which are widely grown as house plants, *Cissus striata* is an evergreen climber originating in South America. It is hardy down to about –7°C (19°F). Its chief attraction is that it is a leafy, luxuriant plant that has beautifully cut leaves. It grows to about 10m (30ft) in ideal conditions. In frost-prone regions it should be grown against a wall where, if it is cut down by severe weather, it may well shoot again. In milder areas it can be grown in cool, damp shade, where it will be protected from frosts. The summer flowers are insignificant but are followed by red to reddish-black, pea-sized berries. *C. striata* has tendrils with suckering pads capable of sticking to walls and trees. It grows in good, moisture-retentive soil and can be cut back in spring or summer if necessary.

CAMPSIS × TAGLIABUANA 'MADAME GALEN' ♀

CELASTRUS ORBICULATUS

CISSUS STRIATA

CLEMATIS

Known as the queen of climbers, no gardener considering climbing plants for their garden can ignore the range of colour and season offered by this genus. Although there are some herbaceous types, most are fully hardy to frost hardy, deciduous or evergreen woody climbers that use leaf stalks to attach themselves to other plants or supports.

CLEMATIS 'KATHLEEN DUNFORD'

Group 1 Early clematis
Starting in winter, this group only needs pruning, if overgrown, after flowering. *C. cirrhosa* has cream- and red-spotted, bell-like flowers against evergreen foliage. Another bold evergreen clematis, *C. armandii* carries clusters of saucer-shaped, perfumed white flowers in early spring. The next to flower are *C. alpina* ♀ and *C. macropetala*, both with blue, bell-shaped flowers followed by silvery fluffy seedheads. There are many

colour variants and hybrids from white to pink, and yellow in *C. koreana*. *C. montana* has single flowers and can grow up to 10m (30ft), covering small trees, pergolas, and fences. This useful plant often has purple tinged young foliage. Also recommended:
C. alpina 'Francis Rivis' ♀
C. armandii 'Apple Blossom'
C. cirrhosa 'Jingle Bells'
C. montana f. *grandiflora* ♀
C. montana 'Elizabeth' ♀

Group 2 Mid-season, large-flowered clematis
In early summer, the large-flowered hybrids flower, sometimes with a few later blooms. There are many colour variants, some with stripes and double-flowered forms. These may be pruned in early spring – it is often enough to thin out old wood. 'Kathleen Dunford' is a prolific, large-flowered hybrid with semi-double flowers. 'Guernsey Cream' has single, large flowers. Easily grown in sun or shade.

CLEMATIS TANGUTICA

CLEMATIS 'GUERNSEY CREAM'

Also recommended:
'Fireworks' ♀
'Gillian Blades' ♀
'Mrs Cholmondeley' ♀
'Niobe' ♀
'Royalty' ♀

Group 3 Late season, large-flowered clematis
In mid- to late summer, late flowering clematis come to the fore, some with small flowers related to the species *C. viticella* and *C. texensis*. These can all be hard pruned to within 30cm (12in) of the ground in late winter or early spring and can be trained to grow through shrubs, or herbaceous plantings. Also flowering in late summer are *C. rehderiana* ♀ and *C. flammula*, with scented blooms, and relatives of *C. tangutica*, which has bell-shaped, yellow flowers followed by attractive seedheads.
Also recommended:
'Jackmanii Superba'
'Gypsy Queen'
'Princess Diana'
'Alba Luxurians'

CLIANTHUS

Clianthus puniceus ♥ is a fairly tender, evergreen, scandent shrub from New Zealand. Although shrubby, it does tend to sprawl and thus needs wires or support from other plants to reach up to 2.5m (8ft). Known sometimes as lobster claw, it produces dangling clusters of giant red, pea-like flowers with a spur-shaped keel and a long upper petal, which gives it this name. These are produced in mid- to late summer. There are other forms in red, white, or pink, but the straight species is the best for colour and performance. Frost hardy, it needs a warm location, such as a sunny wall or fence. It prefers well-drained soils, particularly in winter, when too much damp can cause the stem to rot. In cold districts, cover the plant with an organic mulch, plastic, or straw for protection. Nothing more than an occasional trim should be necessary to keep it tidy.

COBAEA

A tender, evergreen perennial, often woody when mature, *Cobaea scandens* ♥ is usually treated as an annual. Native to Central and South America, the cup and saucer plant is a strong-growing climber up to 5m (15ft). The fragrant greenish-violet to purple flowers are borne on long stalks from the leaf junctions from mid- to late summer. The main flower is a classic bell shape, which is surrounded by a bright green "saucer". It is a lush, twining plant with oval leaves and some tendrils, needing only wires, string, or another plant for support. It likes most moisture-retentive soils and can be grown in sun or partial shade. To grow as an annual, sow seed early in spring in a warm greenhouse and plant out once the risk of late frosts is over. In warmer climates, it will survive over winter. The white-flowered form is less vigorous. Prune back hard in the spring.

DICENTRA

Like its close relation, the herbaceous bleeding heart of borders, *Dicentra macrocapnos* dies down to a fleshy rootstock each winter and has juicy and succulent foliage. The heart-shaped flowers also resemble their herbaceous cousin but are yellow and carried in bunches in summer, lasting until any frosts. It can reach a height of up to 4m (12ft) in the season, covering neighbouring shrubs or wall plants. This is the best way to grow it, as long as the host plants are not too delicate. If room allows, it can be trained through the lower stems of early-flowering rambling roses. The foliage is bluish-green, ferny, and light, with tendrils. The tuberous rootstock is hardy down to –15°C (5°F), and can be protected with straw in winter. It prefers well-drained soil that is not too fertile. *D. scandens* is similar and also herbaceous, but grows only 3m (10ft) each year.

CLIANTHUS PUNICEUS ♥

COBAEA SCANDENS ♥

DICENTRA SCANDENS

DREGEA

Also known as **Wattakaka**, this twining, climbing deciduous plant is suitable only for fairly sheltered gardens or for the conservatory, where it is hardy down to −10°C (14°F). It is closely related to the more tender hoyas. The small, greyish heart-shaped, pointed leaves are downy underneath and are carried on twining stems to about 4m (12ft). Throughout the summer, **Dregea sinensis** produces heads of small, white, starry flowers with tiny red speckles, carried in hanging umbels. These have a lovely scent, which is more apparent when the plant is grown in an enclosed space. In cold regions *D. sinensis* must be grown with the shelter of a wall, in full sun, and needs some protection in winter. It likes any reasonable, well-drained soil and can be grown on wires or any structure without being tied. Prune in spring or after flowering to keep it manageable.

ECCREMOCARPUS

Eccremocarpus scaber ♀ is an almost woody, evergreen, perennial climber reaching up to 3m (10ft) in height, which attaches itself by tendrils. Also known as the Chilean glory flower, it is not fully hardy and may be killed down to the ground at temperatures below −8°C (18°F). Its pinnate leaves have a fern-like grace. The tubular, orange-scarlet flowers are about 3cm (1¼in) long and are carried on long stems bearing 10–20 blooms from summer onwards. In cold regions, Chilean glory flowers are grown as annuals and may flower a little later. Sow seed in late winter in a heated greenhouse and plant out after late frosts. Colours can be selected from seed, from yellow through orange to red. Chilean glory flower is best grown against a wall or through other plants. It likes most soil types except chalk, but prefers those that are acidic and well drained. Cut back in spring.

EUONYMUS

Most euonymus – usually seen as low, evergreen shrubs used as ground cover – spread by aerial roots, which take hold when they touch the ground. However, these aerial roots can attach themselves to walls or the stems of trees, rather like ivy. In **Euonymus fortunei** var. *radicans* this habit is well developed, and plants can climb trees and cliffs to 6m (20ft). The toothed, small, oval leaves cover the plant densely, and have a slight silvery veining. In late summer and autumn, these leaves, although evergreen, turn a deep burgundy-red, making the plant attractive all winter. Flowers and fruit are relatively insignificant. The plant's main assets are its dense, evergreen nature and the fact that it is fully hardy, tolerates any soil type, and grows in dry and shady positions. Pruning is mostly unnecessary. Some variegated forms can be trained on house walls.

DREGEA SINENSIS

ECCREMOCARPUS SCABER ♀

EUONYMUS FORTUNEI VAR. *RADICANS*

FALLOPIA

Often called Russian vine or mile-a-minute, *Fallopia baldschuanica* ♀ is a rampant climber well known for its ability to cover unsightly buildings and fences in a very short period of time. It is a woody deciduous vine, with pointed, heart-shaped leaves that deck the long shoots. It can be a little slow to get started in its first two years but after that the shoots can grow as much as 4m (12ft) in one season. From summer until autumn, the whole plant is covered in a mass of tiny, creamy-white flowers, making it a spectacular sight. It is a twining plant, so it needs something to hold on to in order to get started. Do not plant Russian vine on house walls, because the rampant growth can damage gutters and tiles. It is not fussy as to soil type and is fully hardy, but will flower more readily in a sunny position. Prune hard in late winter.

FICUS

Ficus pumila ♀, the creeping or climbing fig, is an evergreen climber that is related (but shows little resemblance) to the fig. It attaches itself to walls or trees by aerial roots, in much the same way as ivy does, and can reach heights of up to 10m (30ft). *F. pumila* may also grow along the ground like ivy. The leaves start off small and heart shaped but they change to being more fig-like in shape when they reach maturity at the top of a tree or wall. This is a habit that can also be seen in the common ivy. *F. pumila* is hardy down to –8°C (18°F), and makes a useful and handsome evergreen cover. Its flowers are inconspicuous. This is a climber that is easily grown in most soil types, and needs pruning only to maintain a tidy shape. If necessary, do this in early spring. **'Minima'** has small leaves and in **'Variegata'** the leaves are cream margined.

GELSEMIUM

Gelsemium sempervirens ♀ is native to the southern United States, where it is known as the Carolina, or false jasmine. It belongs to a genus of evergreen, twining climbers with small, glossy leaves that carry fragrant, jasmine-like blooms. The five-petalled, trumpet-shaped flowers of *G. sempervirens* are pale to deep yellow and appear from spring to late summer. Growing up to 3m (10ft) or more under ideal conditions, gelsemiums can be pruned immediately after the first flowering in spring when old flowering stems should be thinned out. Gelsemiums grow in any well-drained, fertile soil in full sun but, like many evergreens, must be kept fairly dry during winter. They are frost hardy down to –5°C (23°F) and can be grown outdoors only in mild areas against a warm, sunny wall. In warm climates, gelsemiums can be grown to disguise sheds or fences.

FALLOPIA BALDSCHUANICA ♀

FICUS PUMILA 'VARIEGATA'

GELSEMIUM SEMPERVIRENS ♀

GOURDS (*CUCURBITA*)

Cucurbita pepo
covers a wide
variety of half
hardy, ornamental
gourds, pumpkins,
and marrows.
In general, they
are extremely
useful and
decorative plants, grown
as annuals, and they can be
used to cover fences, arbours,
trellises, and arches.
Gourds enjoy rich soils and
plenty of well-rotted manure
or garden compost and must
be given plenty of water.
Care must be taken not to
overwater them, however,
so plant them on a slight
mound. Grow from seed,
sown in early spring in pots
in a warm greenhouse,
or directly outdoors in late
spring and early summer.
Plant two or three seeds in
each pot. The seeds will
germinate in a few days.
The plants grow vigorously
and may need a lot of space,
some reaching heights of up
to 6m (20ft).

ORNAMENTAL GOURD

drinking vessels. In warm
climates, they may be grown
over an arbour where the
fruits can dangle.

Pumpkins
Some of these familiar, edible,
bright orange fruits reach
proportions that would make
them impossible for climbing.
There are, however, many
small-fruited types that may
be trained upwards.

Squashes and marrows
There are numerous edible
forms of the trailing *C. pepo*
including zucchini (which
can be trained on a tripod of
canes), 'Acorn', 'Hubbards',
'Turk's Turban', and
'Vegetable Spaghetti'.

Cucumbers and gherkins
Belonging to the gourd
family is *Cucumis sativus*, or
cucumber, which can grow to
as much as 5m (15ft) in one
season. Many of these are
suited to outdoors including
'Crystal Lemon', which has
small round fruits and may
be trained up canes.

Ornamental gourds
Often available from seed
companies as mixtures,
varying from egg-shaped to
small, wrinkly, warty, and
stripy yellow and green
fruits. Some are pear-shaped
and others are squat like
miniature pumpkins. These
gourds are inedible.

Bottle gourds
These are long, tapering
green to brown fruits, used in
some parts of the world as

HOLBOELLIA

Holboellia coriacea
is a vigorous,
evergreen, woody
vine reaching a
height of up to 7m
(22ft), suitable for growing
on high walls or trees. It may
need support until it starts to
twine around the wires or
branches. It has luxuriant,
dark green, leathery leaves
made up of three or more
radiating leaflets. It flowers
in spring. The whitish female
flowers are waxy, bell-shaped,
and carried in clusters of up
to ten on new growth. The
male flowers, which are
carried higher up on older
growth, are purple-green. The
main attraction of *H. coriacea*
is its superb fragrance, which
can carry as far as jasmine's –
perhaps the strongest scent of
any reasonably hardy vine.
Native to Western China, it is
hardy down to about –10°C
(14°F), and prefers a moist
root run in shade or semi-
shade. It is a suitable climber
for a cool conservatory. Prune
in late spring after flowering
where necessary.

HOLBOELLIA CORIACEA

HUMULUS

The common hop *Humulus lupulus* is a fully hardy, herbaceous perennial climber,  which dies down to a long-lived rootstock and grows back each year to 8m (25ft) or more. Hops are grown commercially for their papery bracts which, when crushed, add a bitter flavour to beer. The dried flowers may be stuffed into pillows, as a cure for sleeplessness, or cut and dried on their stems and used as decoration (they also absorb the smell of cigarette smoke). The golden-leaved hop, *H. lupulus* 'Aureus' ♀, is the one most often seen in gardens. It does not flower readily, but it has bold foliage. The divided, maple-like leaves can scorch in strong sunshine, but if given too much shade, their colour may revert to green. It is a twining plant, best grown on a pole or up a large tree, in a good, loamy soil with plenty of moisture. In its green form the species is very vigorous. Prune dead growth in spring.

HUMULUS LUPULUS 'AUREUS' ♀

HONEYSUCKLE (*LONICERA*)

Honeysuckles are popular for their fragrant flowers and ease of cultivation. Some are evergreen, and some do not have any fragrance, but all climb by twining their stems around the branches of trees and shrubs. Left alone, they will grow into dense thickets. The flowers are typical throughout the genus, with a small cluster, or whorl, of tubular flowers that are attractive to moths, the main pollinators. Most honeysuckles are fully hardy

LONICERA JAPONICA 'HALLIANA' ♀

and will thrive on all soil types in sun or shade. In hot climates, the roots should be given some shade. Take care that strong-growing forms do not smother nearby plants. Tired plants may be invigorated by removing the old and twiggy growth in winter and cutting old flowering stems back to the main shoots immediately after flowering.

LONICERA PERICLYMENUM 'SEROTINA' ♀

Evergreen or semi-evergreen Japanese honeysuckle, *Lonicera japonica,* reaches up to 10m (30ft) and can be invasive. It roots readily when it trails along the ground. The late-summer flowers are small and cream-coloured, and very fragrant 'Halliana' ♀ and 'Hall's Prolific' are selected cultivars, while 'Aureoreticulata' has yellow veining on its leaves.

Deciduous
L. etrusca reaches 4m (12ft) and has yellow flowers. A native to Europe reaching 7m (22ft) is *L. periclymenum*. It has many forms including 'Belgica' ♀, early Dutch honeysuckle, with pink and red flowers in early summer. 'Serotina' ♀, late Dutch honeysuckle, is similar but flowers in late summer. *L.* × *tellmanniana* ♀ reaches 5m (15ft) and has orange flowers in midsummer. *L. tragophylla* ♀ reaches 6m (20ft) and has yellow flowers in mid- to late summer.

HYDRANGEA

A vigorous, deciduous, self-clinging climber, **Hydrangea anomala** subsp. **petiolaris** ♀ has flowers similar to those of the shrubby hydrangeas. Its large, flat, creamy-white flowerheads are up to 20cm (8in) across and open in early summer, often continuing into late summer. Given a cool aspect, this is a superb climber. It is useful as one of the few climbers suitable for dark, dank, sunless walls. In woodland situations it looks good covering old tree stumps. It is often slow to get going but after the first two or three years, puts on 1m (3ft) of growth or more per year up to 15m (50ft). The main stems and leafy growth cling to the host using stem roots, while the flowering shoots are held away from the stem and are thus shown off well. This hydrangea is hardy down to −10°C (14°F). **H. seemannii** is evergreen but not as hardy as its deciduous relative. Prune, if necessary, after flowering.

HYDRANGEA ANOMALA SUBSP. PETIOLARIS ♀

IVY (HEDERA)

Ivy is a versatile, fully hardy to half hardy, evergreen climber that uses stem roots to cling to trees, rocks, and buildings. It can damage houses built of soft stone or mortar and can prove very invasive in warm climates. Prune in early spring.

Green-leaved ivies
Hedera hibernica ♀, known as Irish ivy, reaches 10m (30ft) and is an effective, fast-growing ground cover plant.

HEDERA COLCHICA 'SULPHUR HEART' ♀

H. canariensis reaches 4m (12ft), is frost hardy and has large, glossy leaves. It is most often seen as variegated **'Gloire de Marengo'** ♀.

Variegated ivies
The great characteristic of ivies is the amazing range of variegation and leaf shape. **H. helix**, or common ivy, reaches 5m (15ft) and is very variable:

HEDERA HIBERNICA

'Buttercup' ♀ (which has bright yellow shoots), **'Goldheart'** (**'Oro di Bogliasca'**), with a central gold splash to the leaf, and **'Glacier'** ♀ (which has a cream edge with a grey and white cast to the leaf giving it an overall cool feel). As with many other ivies, the variegated leaves of **H. canariensis** **'Gloire de Marengo'** ♀ can take on a reddish tinge during the colder months. Fully hardy, with larger leaves are **H. colchica** ♀ (up to 10m/30ft), **'Dentata Variegata'** ♀ (with yellow margins), and **'Sulphur Heart'** ♀ (which has gold markings in the centre).

Ivy flowers and fruits
The small, green flowers are borne only on mature plants. The flowers are produced late in the year, providing food for bees. The blackish fruits that follow are round. **H. helix** f. **poetarum** (Italian ivy) produces yellow fruit.

IPOMOEA

Ipomoea tricolor, or morning glory, is a popular, frost-tender, annual climber, grown for its exquisite sky-blue, trumpet-like flowers. These open in the morning and fade soon after midday, especially in a hot position. Each bloom lasts a very short time, but there is a profuse succession throughout the summer. Growing to 3m (10ft) and thriving in any fertile soil in full sun, *I. tricolor* is a twining climber and often needs only a few strings for support. Sow seed early in spring in a warm greenhouse, and plant out when the night-time temperature is over 10°C (50°F). *I. alba*, or moonvine, is perennial in tropical climates and opens in the evening and at night. Its huge flowers have a lovely fragrance. *I. batatas* 'Blackie' is a purple-leaved form of sweet potato, good for trailing from a pot. Prune in late winter or early spring. All can be invasive in tropical regions.

JASMINUM

The hardiest of the sweet-smelling jasmines, frost hardy **Jasminum officinale** ♀ is a magnificent, semi-evergreen, twining, shrubby climber, with oval leaflets. It rapidly reaches 6m (20ft), growing up to 2m (6ft) in a season. The white flowers, often tinged pink in bud, appear from mid- to late summer. Prune in early spring. *J. officinale* may need the protection of a warm wall in cold areas. In a severe winter, it may be killed to the ground, but will sprout from the base. Jasmines tolerate any soil but prefer full sun. *J. polyanthum* ♀ is half hardy and has more perfumed flowers than those of *J. officinale*. Both have golden-leaved and variegated forms. The yellow, winter-flowering *J. nudiflorum* ♀, fully hardy, is a sprawling shrub, but is often trained on sunless walls. *J. sambac* is a tender, evergreen climber with fragrant blooms.

LAPAGERIA

The national flower of Chile, *Lapageria rosea* ♀ is a lovely, evergreen twiner. Chilean bellflowers are barely frost hardy and, under ideal conditions, can reach 5–6m (15–20ft). From mid- to late summer, they carry the most exquisite, thick, 6cm (2½in) long, waxy bells that reflex slightly at the opening, produced singly and in bunches at the ends of short shoots. They are a beautiful dark pink. There is also a white form, which is less vigorous. Chilean bellflowers can be grown in a greenhouse if the temperature is kept above 0°C (32°F). Outside they prefer a sunny position that is shaded from the hottest sun of the day. Grow in an acid soil that is rich in humus, or ericaceous compost. They also need an ample supply of moisture, and the roots should never dry out. In difficult conditions, Chilean bellflowers can be grown in containers if watered frequently. Prune lightly in early spring.

IPOMOEA ALBA

JASMINUM OFFICINALE
'ARGENTEOVARIEGATUM' ♀

LAPAGERIA ROSEA ♀

MUEHLENBECKIA

A curious, deciduous to semi-evergreen climber, native to New Zealand, this is a useful twining plant with slender, wiry stems. It is excellent for covering old tree stumps or for growing through a wire fence to form a barrier. Capable of reaching 7m (22ft), **Muehlenbeckia complexa** looks good growing up old trees but may become invasive, like its relative, *Fallopia*. The small leaves are fiddle-shaped. The greenish-white flowers, produced in late summer, are of no great significance. **M. complexa** var. ***trilobata*** has more attractive leaves and more vigorous but tidier growth. **M. complexa** 'Nana' is happy in any soil type but best in free-draining, sandy soils. It can be grown in full sun or shade and is fully hardy. **M. axillaris** Walpers, grows to only 50cm (20in), and can be used on small wire frames for topiary. For larger frames, grow **M. complexa**. Prune in early spring.

MUEHLENBECKIA AXILLARIS

PARTHENOCISSUS

Also known as Virginia creeper, this genus is native to the east coast of the United States. ***Parthenocissus quinquefolia*** ♀ is a fully hardy, deciduous, woody climber reaching up to 15m (50ft). It covers trees and buildings with ease, using its adhesive sucker pads. The five-lobed leaves, a soft green in spring, turn a dramatic crimson in the autumn. It is easily grown in almost any soil, in sun or shade. Borderline fully hardy and not as vigorous is the Chinese species **P. henryana** ♀, which has leaf veins picked out in silver. It also turns a glorious red in autumn. **P. tricuspidata** ♀ has ivy-like leaves and is known as Boston ivy. It is fully hardy and has vivid autumn tints. When any of these creepers are grown on buildings, take care that the sucker pads do not damage mortar or stone, and keep them clear of roof tiles and gutters at all times. Prune in autumn or early winter.

PARTHENOCISSUS TRICUSPIDATA ♀

PASSIFLORA

Passiflora caerulea ♀ is a vigorous, frost hardy, evergreen climber. In really cold areas it can be deciduous and may be killed to the rootstock, but should sprout again. In the garden, this passion flower is best grown against a wall. In well-drained, fertile soil in a warm, sheltered site, it will grow to over 12m (40ft). Protect the rootstock with straw in cold areas. The leaves are usually five-lobed and dark green, and the flowers bluish-white to purple. The ten petals are said to represent Christ's disciples; the centre of the flower, the crown of thorns; the five stamens, the wounds; and the three stigmas, the nails. The mid- to late-summer flowers are followed by orange fruits, which in some species are edible (but not in *P. caerulea*). '**Constance Elliot**' ♀ is white-flowered. Most species are tender and suitable for conservatories or for growing in containers over frames. Prune in spring.

PASSIFLORA CAERULEA ♀

PILEOSTEGIA

Pileostegia viburnoides ♀ is in some ways similar to *Hydrangea anomala* subsp. *petiolaris* ♀ to which it is related. A hardy, evergreen, self-clinging climber from China, it attaches itself by aerial roots, but should be given some support to prevent it becoming top heavy and pulling away from a wall. The leaves are long, thick, and a lustrous deep green, making a good foil for the flat heads of creamy-white flowers. These appear in summer and last well into the autumn. It thrives best in some sun and, although it is still happy without sunshine, it will produce fewer flowers. It prefers a fertile, moisture-retentive, acid soil when it can reach up to 5m (15ft). It can be grown over an old tree stump as a mounded plant. There are many occasions when a hardy, evergreen, flowering climber is called for, and few fit the bill as well as pileostegias. Prune in spring for shape, if required.

PLUMBAGO

Cape leadwort is such a familiar plant that the classic blue of its flowers is often used as a benchmark to describe other plants. It is a tough, easy, half-hardy, evergreen plant, with slender stems and oval, light green leaves. The flower heads are pale sky-blue with a grey overtone, borne in clusters at the ends of the branching growth throughout the summer and into autumn. Strictly a scandent shrub, *Plumbago auriculata* ♀ is barely self-supporting, and would form a mound of arching growth if left untrained. It reaches 3–6m (10–20ft), and is often trained up an arch or wall in sheltered, frost-free gardens, or grown as a hedge, or in containers on terraces. It is suited to most soils but needs full sun. In cooler climates, this plant should be overwintered in a cold greenhouse. Regular pruning encourages longer flowering. There are deeper blue forms as well as white.

RHODOCHITON

A tender, evergreen perennial, grown in temperate climates as an annual, *Rhodochiton atrosanguineus* ♀ reaches 2–3m (6–10ft) in full sun or part shade, in any fertile soil. It is perfect for the patio or conservatory or for growing up an arch or a tripod. Like clematis, it climbs by winding the stalks of its heart-shaped leaves, which may be tinted red at the edges, around its host. Usually summer-flowering, it may bloom all year round in ideal conditions. Each flower has curious rose-red outer petals, from which hang a dark red, velvety flower tube. The whole resembles a small umbrella. To grow this as a perennial, overwinter it in a pot, keeping it as dry as possible to prevent stem rot. Cut back to a main framework in the spring. To grow as an annual, sow seeds in early spring in a greenhouse. Prick out the seedlings into a pot and plant when the risk of frost has passed.

PILEOSTEGIA VIBURNOIDES ♀

PLUMBAGO AURICULATA ♀

RHODOCHITON ATROSANGUINEUS ♀

ROSES (*ROSA*)

Climbing and rambling roses are semi-evergreen or deciduous. They need plenty of support from wires, trellis, large obelisks or, in the case of some ramblers, large trees.

Ramblers
Rambling roses, or ramblers, make long arching growths, sometimes up to 4m (12ft) long in a season and flower once only from sideshoots off these stems the following spring. If grown in the open they form an impenetrable thicket often leaving a mass of dead stems inside. Trained on a pergola or large obelisk, old flowering shoots can be thinned out after flowering and new long stems tied in. If grown into a tree there will be little need to attend to them. *Rosa* 'Albertine' ♥ has copper buds opening to fragrant, salmon-pink blooms. 'Crimson Shower' ♥ produces a cascade of beautiful red flowers in midsummer.

'SANDERS' WHITE RAMBLER' ♥

'Sanders' White Rambler' ♥ is a beautiful, fragrant rose. Large growers include: 'Frances E. Lester' ♥ which has pinkish white, fragrant blooms with yellow stamens. 'Rambling Rector' ♥ and 'Wedding Day' are excellent scented white roses. 'Treasure Trove' has scented, apricot flowers and purple-tinted young growth.

Climbing roses
These have stiffer growth than ramblers. Many are repeat flowering. They are pruned to a permanent framework of branches between late autumn and early spring. A few are similar in habit and vigour to the ramblers, including some delightful roses such as 'Maigold' ♥ with a mass of bronze-yellow flowers in early summer and dark green leaves, 'Madame Gregoire Staechelin' ♥, which has pink blooms and dark green leaves, and 'New Dawn' ♥ with its healthy, glossy foliage and shell-pink

fragrant blooms, which may be trained along fencing. More upright climbers suitable for training up pillars, include two strong, single to semi-double, red roses, **Dortmund** ® and **Parkdirektor Riggers** ® with fine, disease-resistant foliage. Climbing versions of hybrid teas also make good pillar roses. '**Climbing Lady Hillingdon**' ♥ has coppery-purple young foliage and fragrant, deep apricot-yellow flowers. '**Climbing Etoile de Hollande**' ♥ has deep red blooms with a fine fragrance. Like hybrid teas, these are best pruned in late winter or early spring.

All of these roses have similar requirements. A rich loam suits them well with plenty of water at the beginning of the growing season. A generous mulch of well-rotted manure in the autumn or spring will act as a feed and will help conserve moisture and suppress weeds.

'CRIMSON SHOWER' ♥

'ALBERTINE' ♥

RUBUS

These hardy ornamental brambles are relatives of the blackberry and raspberry. They are capable of climbing over shrubs and into trees, using their stout prickles as anchorage. In the garden they are likely to be trained on wires or walls, and will need to be tied to supports with twine. All grow easily in sun or shade, in any reasonable soil. The tips of growing shoots often root when they touch the ground. *Rubus phoenicolasius*, known as the Japanese wineberry, is covered in red bristles and has red, sticky, and slightly tart-tasting fruit in late summer. It may be planted in the flower garden, trained on posts or against a wall. *R. henryi* grows vigorously to 5m (15ft), and has dark green foliage, which is white-felted beneath. The variety *bambusarum* is similar but smaller growing. Prune in late winter or early spring to promote growth.

SCHISANDRA

Schisandra rubriflora is a deciduous, twining, shrubby climber reaching up to 6m (20ft), which is chiefly grown for its lovely, red flowers produced in late spring to summer. These hang singly from the leaf junctions when in bud. It is worth trying to grow it for the fruits as well. The male and female flowers are carried separately on the same plant, but sometimes on separate plants, so there is no guarantee that plants will bear the red, currant-like fruits. Some sources offer sexed plants. A male and female may be planted close together to encourage pollination and fruiting. Hardy to –20°C (–4°F), schisandras prefer fertile, moisture-retentive soil in partial shade. They can be grown over a pergola, through other plants and small trees, or on a wall, supported by wires. Prune in late winter to early spring. *S. sphenanthera* has orange flowers in late spring to early summer and oval foliage.

SCHIZOPHRAGMA

Another relative of the hydrangea, *Schizophragma hydrangeoides* ♀ is a self-clinging, deciduous, hardy plant that needs a wall or tree to scale. The leaves are rounded and coarsely toothed, and turn bright yellow in autumn. The flowers are produced in midsummer and are borne in flattened, lacy heads surrounded by a ring of conspicuous, diamond-shaped, creamy-white bracts. These remain on the plant for many weeks. Growing to up to 5m (15ft) and hardy to –20°C (–4°F), schizophragmas like some sun to ensure a good flower display, and any reasonable soil rich in humus. Less vigorous schizophragmas are 'Roseum' (which has rose-coloured bracts) and 'Moonlight' (with mottled leaves veined in silver-grey). *S. integrifolium* ♀ is larger but slow to get going. It can be grown over an old tree stump to form a mound. Prune, if necessary, after flowering.

RUBUS HENRYI
VAR. *BAMBUSARUM*

SCHISANDRA RUBRIFLORA

SCHIZOPHRAGMA
INTEGRIFOLIUM ♀

SOLANUM

Solanums are strictly shrubs, but are almost always treated in the same way as climbers – they would otherwise form lax mounds (and may be grown as such). For the most part, they need the protection afforded by a wall, and their wandering growth is best tied in to wires or a trellis. Hardy to –10°C (14°F) and best in soil that is not too rich or alkaline, solanums may reach 5m (15ft). *S. crispum* (related to the potato and native to Chile and Peru) has arching, scandent, semi-evergreen growth carrying large clusters of fragrant, light violet flowers with orange stamens in early summer. **'Glasnevin'** ♥ is outstanding – its flowers have a rich colour and long season. *S. laxum* has fragrant, blue flowers but is half-hardy. Its white form, **'Album'** ♥, is a wonderful sight in full flower. It is a fast climber, and can cover a 2–3m (6–10ft) wall in one season. Prune in early spring or after flowering.

SOLLYA

Sollya heterophylla ♥ is a small, tender, twining, evergreen climber from Australia that is suitable for a well-sheltered position in a mild area. It should be grown in a well-drained, moist, lime-free soil, rich in organic matter. Reaching around 2–3m (6–10ft), it has small, delicate leaves and, in summer, produces sprays of nodding, 1cm (½in) long, bell-shaped flowers of a beautiful sky-blue. Although they are frost hardy, sollyas suffer from the cold and become untidy-looking. If grown on an obelisk or a tripod in a container, their flowering season can be prolonged by overwintering in a warm greenhouse, at 10°C (50°F) or more, and then being placed outside in a sunny position, in summer. In a container, they need well-drained lime-free compost with some loam. Prune only for shape in spring, when new growth starts to break. There is also a pink-flowered form.

THUNBERGIA

Well known as black-eyed Susan (a name also attributed to *Rudbeckia*), **Thunbergia alata** has very decorative, orange-yellow flowers with black centres. Native to South Africa, it is a tender, evergreen, perennial vine that may flower almost all year if kept above 10°C (50°F) and is hardy down to 3°C (37°F). It has soft, hairy growth, up to 2m (6ft) in a season, with heart-shaped leaves. Flower colour varies from white to shades of yellow. **'Moonglow'** is a luminous pale peach. **'Molly'** is a hybrid, with butter-yellow flowers. In cold climates *T. alata* is grown in a conservatory or treated as an annual, grown in a pot on a tripod of canes or through other plants in a border. Sow seed in spring in a heated greenhouse, and prick out into small pots before planting out in early summer, in a sunny site with reasonable soil. Prune after flowering.

SOLANUM CRISPUM **'GLASNEVIN'** ♥

SOLLYA HETEROPHYLLA ♥

THUNBERGIA ALATA

SWEET PEAS (*LATHYRUS*)

Hardy perennials

The perennial peas climb by the use of tendrils and may be trained on wires or over a wigwam of twigs, or grown through hedges and shrubs, or left to sprawl over the ground in a mound. The flowers are rosy-purple, often with many to a stem, and bloom throughout late summer. In hot summers or dry regions, some shade and moisture are preferable. Almost any soil is suitable. Prune after flowering in autumn or early spring.

Lathyrus latifolius ♀ is fully hardy and reaches 2m (6ft). It has winged leaf stems and

LATHYRUS LATIFOLIUS ♀

shoots. **'White Pearl'** ♀ and **'Albus'** ♀ have extra-large, white flowers. **'Rosa Perle'** ♀ has pink flowers.

L. grandiflorus has some of the fragrance of the annual. It is fully hardy and reaches 1.5m (5ft) in height.

Annual sweet peas

L. odoratus ♀ is the well-known sweet pea, a fully

LATHYRUS ODORATUS BIJOU GROUP

hardy, annual climbing plant that reaches up to 2m (6ft). It is grown for its fragrant flowers carried on long stalks in many colours. A vase of sweet peas will scent an entire room. Cutting the flowers encourages the plant to produce more. Left uncut, they may go to seed early and the plant will stop producing. Sweet peas are best grown on fertile soils with plenty of organic matter and moisture, and can be trained over walls, up wigwams, or along strings. In autumn, sow one or two seeds in a 9cm (3½in) pot in a seed or potting-based compost. Where winters are severe, overwinter in a cold greenhouse or cold frame. In early spring, sweet peas may be planted out or direct sown in well-prepared soil. Harden off the seedlings before planting them out. Feed regularly. Seed companies list sweet peas of many colours but not all have perfume.

TRACHELOSPERMUM

This is one of the best all-round climbers. Frost hardy, evergreen, woody, and twining, *Trachelospermum jasminoides* ♀ grows to 6m (20ft). The dark green, glossy leaves are leathery, oval, and tapering. The white flowers, similar to periwinkle in shape with a jasmine-like fragrance, are borne in midsummer. The growth is quite dense, so it is suitable for growing on a house wall near a doorway, where its tidy growth and fragrance will be appreciated. It will need support when grown against a wall. Trachelospermums like a well-drained soil that is not too alkaline. They are best kept away from cold winds, but will tolerate seaside locations. Grow against a warm wall in full sun for best results. An attractive but less vigorous variegated form has cream markings on the leaves. *T. asiaticum* ♀ is smaller and can be grown in a container. Prune in early spring.

TRACHELOSPERMUM JASMINOIDES ♀

VINES (*VITIS*)

Ornamental vines

Originating in Japan, **Vitis coignetiae** ♀ is a deciduous, hardy climber. The leaves are up to 30cm (12in) long, heart-shaped at the base and narrowing at the tip. In summer, they are dark green with a rusty felted underside. The leaves turn shades of orange, vermillion, and claret in the autumn. Growing up to 20m (70ft), this vine needs to be carefully placed. It is hardy to temperatures well-below freezing. Other species include *V. amurensis,* which grows to 10m (30ft) and is similar to *V. coignetiae.* *V. davidii* has large, textured leaves and soft, fleshy thorns. *V. aestivalis* is a tree-climber, reaching up to 8m (25ft).

Grape vines

The European grape vine, *V. vinifera*, has been cultivated for thousands of years. It is fully hardy and a long-lived plant, but the fruit

VITIS VINIFERA 'PURPUREA' ♀

does not always ripen well in cold climates. Although cultivated in poor, dry, and gravelly soils for wine production, grapes should be planted in a deep, sandy loam in full sun for best results. Grape vines are ideal for covering arbours over terraces, climbing on wires and other plants to provide shade, and can reach up to 7m (22ft) in height. For fruit production they should be trained on a trellis system for easy maintenance. There are hundreds of varieties – some for wine production and others for eating. Select a variety that best suits your climate. Favoured among the dessert grapes are *V. vinifera* **Black Hamburgh** and 'Brandt' ♀. Of those grown for ornament, *V. vinifera* 'Purpurea' ♀ has grey leaves that turn purple in the summer and claret in the autumn. *V. vinifera* 'Incana' has woolly, white shoots and leaves. Both carry small bunches of purple grapes. Prune in midwinter.

VITIS COIGNETIAE ♀

TROPAEOLUM

The genus **Tropaeolum** includes deciduous, herbaceous perennial climbers and the tender annual nasturtium, *T. majus.* The perennials grow mostly from fleshy tubers. Frost-hardy *T. speciosum* ♀ requires a cool, peaty root run, allowing frail stems with rich green, lobed leaves to climb shrubs or walls, reaching up to 3m (10ft). The small, scarlet, nasturtium-like flowers are carried for weeks in summer. This plant grows well in acid soil on the shady side of evergreen shrubs, such as rhododendrons, or on yew hedges, where the scarlet flowers are shown off well. Frost-hardy *T. polyphyllum* prefers warm but loamy soil, where its foliage can trail up to 1m (3ft), through plants, carrying bright yellow flowers in early summer. The growth dies away after flowering. Half-hardy *T. tuberosum* and 'Ken Aslett' ♀ have orange and red flowers.

TROPAEOLUM SPECIOSUM ♀

TWEEDIA

Tweedia caerulea ♀ is a slender, evergreen, twining climber. It has beautiful, narrow, soft grey-green leaves covered in a fine, downy felt. The flowers, produced in summer, are a remarkable blue – a kind of azure to electric blue with a touch of green or turquoise – a colour rarely found in the plant world. The five-petalled and star-shaped flowers are perfectly complimented by the foliage. They last a long time but fade to a purple-lilac colour. A small plant growing only to 1m (3ft), *T. caerulea* is half-hardy. In mild areas it can be planted outside in a sunny, open site. Elsewhere it can be grown in a frost-free greenhouse or in a container placed outside in a sunny position during the summer, where it will flower until autumn. If planting in a container, use a compost mixed with some loam and plenty of crocks for good drainage. Prune in early spring.

TWEEDIA CAERULEA ♀

WISTERIA

One of the most beautiful of all climbers, wisteria is a vigorous, fully hardy, deciduous, twining plant reaching a height of up to 30m (100ft). It is well known for its elegant, pendulous chains of scented, violet-blue flowers. The two best-known species are *Wisteria floribunda*, from Japan, which twines clockwise, and *W. sinensis* ♀, from China, which twines anti-clockwise. They are similar in many respects. The latter has varieties with the longest flower clusters. Wisterias prefer a good, deep loam with plenty of moisture. Once well established, they can tolerate quite dry conditions. They will need plenty of stout supports if grown on a house wall. Once the plant has gripped a support, its stem continues to expand and will break any weak trellising or guttering.

WISTERIA BRACHYBOTRYS 'SHIRO-KAPITAN'

Wisteria in the garden
Wisterias are ideal for planting over an arbour or pergola, where the flowers will hang down through the foliage cover. There are many varieties available. There are white and pink forms of both species and some of a deeper purple-blue.
W. floribunda 'Multijuga' ♀ has long flower chains.
W. brachybotrys 'Shiro-kapitan' is less well-known and shorter-flowered. Its white flowers open a few weeks earlier than those of *W. sinensis*. Although deciduous, old specimens can be stunning with their gnarled stems. Wisterias can be trained up a single strong pole as a standard. The plant is allowed to twist around two or three times and then branch out at 2–3m (6–10ft) where it forms a cascading head up to 4m (12ft) across. Prune in midwinter and in summer, after flowering.

WISTERIA FLORIBUNDA

INDEX

Page numbers in *italics* indicate illustrations.

ACKNOWLEDGMENTS

Picture research Anna Grapes
                  Mariana Sonnenberg
Picture librarians Richard Dabb

Catalogue illustrations Claire Pegrum

Index Chris Bernstein

Dorling Kindersley would like to thank:
All staff at the RHS, in particular Susanne Mitchell, Karen Wilson and Barbara Haynes at Vincent Square. Thanks also to Joanna Chisholm for editorial assistance.

Studio Cactus would like to thank: Alison Bolus, Sue Gordon, and Kate Hayward for editorial assistance; Lesley Malkin for proofreading; Claire Pegrum, Ann Thompson, and Laura Watson for design assistance. Thanks also to Mr and Mrs Lunn, Mr and Mrs Rudd, and Mr and Mrs Trown for the use of their gardens.

The Royal Horticultural Society
To learn more about the work of the Society, visit the RHS on the internet at **www.rhs.org.uk**.

Information offered includes plant news, horticultural events around the country, RHS Plant Finder, a garden finder, international plant registers, results of plant trials, a gardening calendar and monthly topics of interest, publications and membership details.

Photography
The publisher would also like to thank the following for their kind permission to reproduce their photographs:
(key: t=top, c=centre, b=below, l=left, r=right)
New photography by Damien Moore of Studio Cactus.
Jonathan Buckley: 73bc.
Garden Picture Library: Friedrich Strauss 20bl, 21tl; Lamontagne 70bl.
John Glover: 24tr, 24bl.
Jacqui Hurst: 3bl, 3br, 8br, 9tl, 11tl, 12bl 14bl, 16bl, 19t, 71br, back jacket c.
Andrew Lawson: 13tl.
Harry Smith Collection: 7bl, 15tl, 59br, 61br, 64bl, 64br, 69bl; DG 5541 66tc.